THE
MINNESINGER OF GERMANY

BY

A. E. KROEGER

NEW YORK

PUBLISHED BY HURD AND HOUGHTON

Cambridge: The Riberside Press

LONDON:

TRÜBNER & CO., 8 & 60, PATERNOSTER ROW

1873

Entered according to act of Congress, in the year 1872, by
A. E. KROEGER,
in the Office of the Librarian of Congress, at Washington.

RIVERSIDE, CAMBRIDGE :
PRINTED BY H. O. HOUGHTON AND COMPANY.

To

MY DEAR FRIEND

WILLIAM R. WALKER,

This Book

IS DEDICATED.

CONTENTS.

THE
MINNESINGER OF GERMANY.

CHAPTER I.

THE MINNESINGER AND THE MINNESONG.

ONG before Chaucer had fathered English poetry, and Spain and Italy had developed their languages to that purity which alone makes possible great achievements in the literary arts, Germany had passed through a period of splendor in the art of poetry, which even the period of the last century has not surpassed, and in some respects scarcely equaled. It was in the twelfth and thirteenth centuries, under the glorious reign of the Hohenstauffens, amidst the turmoil of the Crusades, and whilst the sublime conceptions of the cathedrals of Strassburg and Cologne were being wrought out, that there sprang up in Germany, as if by magic, that wonderful craft of Minnesinger, which lasted throughout a century and then gradually expired ; the grace and beauty of their singing appearing no more in German literature until Goethe struck anew the old tone, and thus heralded the dawn of the second brilliant period of German poetry. Perhaps it was the fact that the

German language is an original tongue, and hence needed not to wait, like the English, Spanish, Italian, and French, for a thorough amalgamation, which made possible this earlier development of literature.

Of these poetical achievements of Germany in the miscalled Dark Ages, only the epic poetry is represented in English literature. The two great national German epics — the *Niebelungen* and the *Kudrun* — are perhaps as familiar as foreign poetry of any kind can ever hope to become to a public so clannish in its literary pursuits, as that which speaks the English language. But of the German lyrical poetry of those ages, and their narrative epics, little or nothing is known outside of Germany, and even there these most wonderful productions of German genius are by no means so widely known as they deserve to be. For that which is surprising in these works, and must make them of perennial value, is their perfection of form, not only in regard to the development of the subject, but also in regard to metre, rhythm, and rhyme. Not Goethe and Schiller, not even Rückert and Platen-Hallermünde have attained that utmost perfection of rhyme which characterizes Gottfried von Strassburg, Walther von der Vogelweide, Johann Hadloub, and a hundred other poets of those "dark ages ; " and their invention of metres and their ear for the flow of rhythm finds a parallel only in German musicians.

Tennyson and Swinburne of all modern poets — Shelley, too, in some of his lyrics — come nearest to the Minnesinger in melodious sound of words, artful construction of rhythm, and arrangement of stanzas ;

but they lack the fresh, youthful, inexpressibly sweet and graceful — because natural — flow of form, and the still more charming naïve subjects of the Minnelied. Jacob Grimm calls the Minnelieder a womanly poetry, and justly enough ; though in the works of Walther von der Vogelweide, the greatest of the Minnesinger, there are poems of the manliest character. But, on the whole, these Minnelieder breathe indeed nothing but love and sweetness ; love and sweetness of the woods, meadows, flowers, grass, rivers, and birds ; love and sweetness of woman ; and love and sweetness of Mary, the Mother of God.

It was the German poet Bodmer who first, in 1748, discovered and made known again the immense wealth of this early German literature, which for some centuries had been lost and swamped in the prosaic poetry of the Meistersinger and their successors ; and it is chiefly through the untiring exertions of Friedrich Heinrich von der Hagen, in the commencement of this century, that most of its treasures have been brought to light and made accessible. The generous support extended to him by King Frederic William III. of Prussia, enabled him in 1838 to publish that collection in five volumes, which is one of the finest examples of German literary workmanship.

In the middle of the twelfth century, — or about 1150, — this first period of German literature may be said to have begun. Under the Hohenstauffen dynasty the Swabian form of the German language had become the language of all cultured men, and by its mellow sound was indeed peculiarly adapted to the requirements of poetry. The opening of the Orient, through the Crusaders on the one hand, and the spreading of the tales of King Arthur's Round Table, intermingled with those of Charlemagne, on the other, had roused over all Germany a spirit of poetry, to which the language was now fully adapted to give expression. Knights, princes, and kings — the most exposed to this spirit of romance — were seized with it, and studied the intricacies of rhythm or rhyme with the same energy they devoted to their pursuits of war. Duke Leopold of Austria, Landgrave Herrmann of Thüringen, Margrave Henry of Meissen, Duke Henry of Breslau, Duke John of Brabant, King Wenzel of Bohemia, King Conrad, and the Emperor Henry, are among those, some of whose poems have been preserved. Even the great Frederic Barbarossa (Red-beard) — whom tradition reports still sleeping in the Kyffhäuser cave, his head on his hand, and his beard grown all round the table of stone, where he awaits the coming of the new glory of united Germany, — even he, and his perhaps still greater successor, Frederic II., often, after the day of battle or hunting, struck the lyre in their tents or castles, and poured forth those sweet songs of love, that made soldiers, servants, and knights gather to listen. When it is considered that these Minnesinger, these warblers of love, were for the greater part unable to read or write, — even Wolfram von Eschenbach could not read or write, and Ulrich von Lichtenstein had to carry a letter from his sweetheart for weeks in his pocket, before he found some one to read it for him ; that we, therefore, owe almost all our knowledge of their songs to tradition, and that, nevertheless, songs from over one hundred and sixty Minnesinger within that one century have been preserved to us, the extraordinary development of poetical art in that century may be imagined. Most of these Minnesinger were knights, and called Sirs; some of them, however, citizens, whose distinctive appellation was Master. It is Sir (Herr) Walther von der Vogelweide ; and Master (Meister) Gottfried von Strassburg. These singers led a life most strange and romantic. At a time when cities had as yet barely come into existence in Germany, and the castles of the lords were the chief gathering-places of the vast floating population of the crusading times, these Minnesinger with little or nothing besides their sword, fiddle, or harp, and some bit of love-ribbon or the like from their sweetheart, wandered from village to village and castle to castle, everywhere welcomed with gladness, and receiving their expected remuneration with the proud unconcern of strolling vagabonds. Throngs gathered to hear their songs, retained them in memory, and transmitted them to the succeeding generation. One of the chief resorts of the Minnesinger was the castle of Landgrave Herrmann of Thüringen, who was to that century what the Duke of Weimar was to the age of Goethe and Schiller, and whose Castle Wartburg was thus the home of song and literary development long before it became famous as the place where Luther translated the Bible, and by doing so gave rise to a new German language, more vigorous and extensive than that of the Minnesinger, but less fragrant with sensuous beauty and grace. Worthily, therefore, is Landgrave Herrmann

celebrated in the poetry of his numerous guests, as
above all hosts the most hospitable and generous.
For these singing knights felt no more delicacy in
chronicling the good things they received from their
patrons than in immortalizing the meanness of those
who let them depart without gifts of clothing, food,
and money. Yet their lady-loves' names they never
mentioned ; the tender delicacy observed by Don
Quixote, the last of the famous race, was the rule that
governed all. Like him, most of them had their
Sancho Panza in the shape of a youth to whom
alone they intrusted their secret. The chief occupa-
tion of those sweet youths was to commit to memory
the verses which their masters composed for their
mistresses, and, if unable to write, kept repeating to
their Singerlein till he had every word and tone of it
in mind. For he must learn not only the song itself,
but also the melody of it. Then this living letter
would be dispatched to the beauteous Dulcinea, who
would listen attentively with due German sentimen-
tality, and having had it sung to her until she could
again repeat it perhaps to others, would give the
young starved Singerlein a glass of wine and piece of
bread, and mayhap other luxuries for himself and his
master. It is thus chiefly through oral tradition that
there has been preserved to us the immense labors of
a century which the noble Swiss knight, Rüdiger of
Manesse, and his son, first undertook to collect and
fix into manuscript ; thus, under the editorship of
Johann Hadloub, one of the last of the Minnesinger,
arranging that famous Manessian collection which
now forms one of the treasures of the Parisian library,

and which, through Bodmer, first became known again to German literature. The life of Walther von der Vogelweide, as sketched in another chapter, will represent in some measure the average life of the nobler knight-minstrel in the earlier part of the Minnesong period ; whilst the life of Ulrich von Lichtenstein, also sketched herein, will illustrate the more extravagant form of knight-minstrelsy, and show how little Cervantes had need to exaggerate in his immortal Don Quixote.

Such a knight began his career after his seventh year, when he entered the service of some knight or prince as a page, learning all the accomplishments of a true knight and gentleman, and particularly devotion to the ladies and the holy cause of religion. At the age of fourteen he assumed a sort of independent existence at his lord's castle, but it was not until he reached his twenty-first year that he was solemnly installed into the order of knights. This ceremony being concluded, the young knight was by custom compelled to saunter forth into the world, and generally by poverty to keep on sauntering in this fashion all his life-time. Then he perfected himself in the art of composing songs and playing some stringed instrument, which became both a source of infinite enjoyment, and an unfailing source of revenue if the knight was poor. With his art he paid his boarding-bills ; his art furnished him with clothes, horses, and equipments. More than all, his art won him the love of his lady.

How this art became cultivated amongst these unlettered knights to a degree — far higher than ever

attained by the Provençal poets — that they could
dash off impromptu songs, not only of the most intricate rhythmical and metrical construction, which, to
be sure, Greek poets also may have done, but also of
an equally intricate construction of rhyme, which the
Greek poets made no use of, — such a song, for instance, as Ulrich von Lichtenstein's "To the Beloved," — and generally accompanied with an original
musical air, which must also have been artistically
wrought, or it could not be retained in memory to fit
every strophe of the poem, seems a marvel. Nor are
their narrative poems less wondrous in general unity
of plan, elaborately worked out under-plots, beauty of
diction, and a most peculiar charm of rhythmical construction.

This thorough comprehension and mastery of all
the resources of rhyme and rhythm, which the Minnesinger acquired and which characterizes them, must
appear even in the translated specimens here given,
all of which have been translated so as to retain all
the peculiarities of the rhythm, metre, and rhyme of
the originals. The rare gift and thorough knowledge
of their art, which these men had, must appear to us
almost miraculous ; particularly when the spontaneity
is considered with which their poems with musical
accompaniment were created, and at the same time
the strictness of their art-forms is kept in view. For
every Minnesong — and this is its distinctive feature in
form — has a triplicity of strophe-form ; each strophe
being divided into three parts, the first two corresponding perfectly with each other in the slightest matter
of rhythm and rhyme, and the third forming a rhyth-

mically and metrically connected, but otherwise independent part. In other words, each stanza has its
strophe, anti-strophe, and epode ; and this triplicity
was, in the mature times of Minnepoetry, *never* departed from. In this triplicity of form the German
Minnelied has its originality ; for the looser construction of the Minne-Say and the form of the metrical
romances, the Provençal poets have in common with
the Minnesinger. Now it is not an easy matter to
improvise even a loosely-versed poem ; how much
more difficult, then, to improvise poems such as are
here given! To this must be added, that every new
poem required a new strophe-form ; indeed, to use
the same kind of verse for two different poems, was
considered very inartistic, and no poet was allowed
to use the strophe-form of another.

The first Minnelieder seem to have been all songs
of only one strophe ; Veldeke was probably the first
to connect several strophes into one general song.
Still the song had in the earlier days of the Minnesinger only a very limited number of strophes, rarely
more than five, most frequently two or three. It was
only as the later poets, Nithart, Frauenlob, etc., arose,
that this distinctive trait of the *Minnelied* vanished
with all its other sweet features. The fact that origi-
nally every strophe was a poem by itself, must be
remembered very often to explain a disconnectedness
.in the various strophes of a song, and serves also to
point out the relation as well as the distinction between the form of the *Minnelied* and the *Spruch*.

"To sing and to say :" this expression occurs in
most varied forms throughout the songs of the *Minne-*

lieder, and signifies the two modes in which the Minnesinger gave utterance to their poetic productions. If such a production was a real *Minnelied*, a song of love, the seasons, or feelings, it was invariably composed with its melody and *sung;* but if it was a didactic poem it was simply *spoken*, and hence called *Spruch*, Saying. In so far, therefore, both class of poems were distinguished simply by their contents. But they had also important distinctions of form. Firstly, the *Spruch* retained the form of one strophe for each poem, which the *Minnelied*, as we have seen, discarded; secondly, the various *Sprüche* or Sayings of one poet, could be composed by him in one common tone or strophe-form ; whereas each new *Minnelied* required, as before said, a new tone and melody — at least this rule was so rarely violated, that some *twelve hundred different strophe-forms* have come down to us from the poets of those days ; and thirdly, within the strophe-form the Saying, by reason of being spoken, was allowed liberties of rhythmical changes which to the sung *Lied* were strictly prohibited. Nor did the Saying strictly observe the triplicity of the strophe-form, but often built up its strophe in a very irregular fashion.

Amongst the finest Sayings, those of Walther von der Vogelweide justly claim supremacy, and the following examples will sufficiently illustrate the noble use he made of this form of poetry, as well as the metrical skill he lavished upon its external beautifying : —

EQUALITY BEFORE GOD.

Who without fear, O God, our Lord,
Thy ten commandments speaks by word
And breaketh them : his is not true love, surely.
Thee many a one doth Father name,
But who me not their brother claim :
They speak strong words with sickly mind and poorly.
We have from equal things arisen ;
Food feedeth us, and must us pleasen
When through the mouth its way is laid.
Who could the master from the servant summon,
If he their naked bones saw merely,
Though he in life had known them nearly,
Now that the worms their flesh had preyed ?
Jews, Christians, pagans, worship Him in common,
Who all the living things has made.

MORNING PRAYER.

With thy grace let me rise to-day,
Lord God, in thy protection stay
Wherever o'er the land I ride or wander !
Christ, upon me be pleased t'incline
The great power of that goodness thine,
And keep me well for thy dear mother yonder !
As when the angel kept from danger
Thee, when lying in the manger
Young as man and old as God,
Before the ass and ox, by humblest hedges ;
And as good Joseph then attended,
And upon thee and her there spended

Rare love and fidelity :
Thus do attend Thou me, Lord, that thy pledges
    May also be approved in me.

THE LAST JUDGMENT.

I hear that all the wise men say
There 's close at hand a judgment-day,
Than which was ne'er one known of equal rigor.
    There shall the Judge off-hand declare :
    " No pawn or trust is taken here ! "
Ah ! many a heart will then with fear beat quicker.
    This, lady, aid me here to settle,
    Since none trust there, e'er so little,
        Through that sainted joy of thine,
Which to thine ear the holy angel brought thee,
    With blessed word, to thee revealer
    That thou shouldst bear the sick world's healer,
        To whom our soul all hopes does join.
Who, from the first, to that joy linked in thought
        thee,
    When my end comes, be comfort mine !

GOD'S INSCRUTABILITY.

Almighty God, Thou art so long, Thou art so broad !
Kept we this but in mind always, our labor's load
Would be much lightened ; for thy power and endless
        glory, God,
No thought can scan.   I know't by me ; and though
        men still keep trying :

Thus is it, and thus was it ; and to no mind e'er is
    showed.
Thou art too great, Thou art too small for thought's
    vain spying ;
And fool is he, who days and nights wastes in a pry-
    ing
Into what never yet was preached, or dogma made
    applying.

SELF–CONTROL.

Who slays the lion? who slays the giant ?
Who masters them all, however defiant ?
He does it, who himself controlleth ;
And every nerve of his body enrolleth,
    Freed from passion, under strict subjection.
Mere borrowed manner and shame for a stranger
May glitter awhile ; but here 's the danger :
    The glitter soon expires ; then there 's no action.

In their songs the Minnesinger employed three
kinds of rhyme : (1) the masculine ; (2) the feminine ;
and (3) the rhyme of such duosyllabic endings as are
not in pronunciation given the full value of two syllables. For instance, *Sagen,* pronounced as *Sag'n ;*
or in English, Saying, Heaven, etc. ; words that give
not to the last syllable the full time value of one. As
a rule this last class of rhymes were counted equal to
monosyllabic rhymes, but by no means invariably.
In my translations I have allowed myself the same
freedom, choosing for them, as often as possible,
English equivalents, or else treating them as mascu-

line or feminine rhymes at pleasure. It may be mentioned, that in the first days of Minnepoetry, in the earlier part of the twelfth century, only masculine rhymes were made use of; but the genius of the language soon led to rhymes of two and even three syllables; rhymes that thus interest, not merely from an accidental sameness of sound in the often merely inflected final syllable of a word, but that seem to be produced by a relation in the words themselves, in their very roots.

The ability with which the Minnesinger utilized all possibilities of rhyme is perfectly amazing. Limited to rhymes of complete purity to such an extent that in all of Vogelweide's poems, for instance, only two slight impurities occur, they enlisted the vast resources of their beautiful and flexible language to the utmost extent. We have Minnesongs wherein every word of every line rhymes with the other, while the lines again rhyme in the usual way amongst themselves ; poems wherein the last word of the line is rhymed by the first of the next line ; poems wherein the last word of the strophe rhymes with its first word ; poems built in strophes of twenty and more rhymes ; poems of grammatical rhymes, in the most various possibilities ; poems of word-playing rhymes, etc. ; and in most cases the fundamental rhythmical beauty reigns supreme and makes the ornamentation seem natural outgrowth. Frauenlob has achieved real wonders in this way.

Of these grammatical rhymes, some are employed so as to bring together into one strophe all the flections, moods, tenses, etc., of a word, its various phases as a noun, verb, adjective, etc., collecting, indeed, with all the liberty the genius of the language would permit, its many and different significances by means of rhyme and alliteration. Dr. Wallace's well-known poem, " When a twister a twisting will twist him a twist," exhibits somewhat the manner in which this was done. But quite as often the grammatical lines are simply ingenuous play, as in the following very neat one, also by Walther, where each strophe has as its rhyme end one of the vowels, the five following each other in regular succession. In the translation of such a poem much allowance is, of course, expected; particularly as in the vowels *i* and *u* the English language has really nothing to offer. The Toberlu in the last strophe was a famous cloister of that time.

It will be noticed that this Minnesong has *not* a triplicity of strophe-form. This fact stamps it as one of the poet's earliest productions.

DREARINESS OF WINTER.

Gay looked the field's regalia,
Green bloomed oak and acacia,
Birds warbled their sweet opera,
But now the crows cry their ka, ka !
Gone 's the world's ambrosia,
It seems a pale, gray nebula ;
Men frown at these phenomena.

I sat on a hill beneath a tree,
Where flowers and clover, tall and wee,

Grew up 'tween a sea and me.
That fair scene now no more I see,
Where we then plucked flowers in glee,
Now snow and sleet reach to the knee ;
Sweet bird, this hurts both me and thee.

The fools shout loud : " Snow, snow, hi, hi ! "
The poor mumble : " Ah mi !   Ah mi ! "
Me it seems like alkali.
'Gainst winter three great griefs raise I,
Soon I'd crush these tyranni,
As did the earth fair Pompeii,
If Summer would but come — ah mi !

Rather than lead this life I'll go
And eat raw crabs fore'er.   Heigho !
Summer, come and quench my woe !
Ay, clothe thy fields, that to and fro
I with flowers may play as tho'
What time my heart leapt sunhigh.   Lo,
Now winter 's come ; it leaps no mo'.

I look so Esau-like, perdu,
My hair hangs rough and unkempt.   Hu !
Gentle Summer, where are you ?
Ah, were the world no more so dhu !
Rather than in this purlieu
Longer to stay I'll say, adieu !
And go as monk to Toberlu.

A pretty instance of rhyming the end word of each
strophe with its first word is given in the following
little poem, which also has a refrain, slightly chang-

ing in the last line of each strophe, and which is ascribed to Lady Winsbecke. Whether there ever was such a poetess amongst the Minnesinger is quite doubtful ; her naming has occurred in this fashion : Amongst the Minnelieder there are two quite long poems, the one containing the instructions of a father to his son, and the other those of a mother to her daughter, named respectively ". Der Winsbecke " and "Die Winsbecken," and ascribed to a knight and lady in the portraits that accompany the Manessian collection of Minnelieder. These poems were very popular, and justly so at the time they were written, somewhere in the first part of the thirteenth century, and have been much admired since ; but the author or authors have never been definitely ascertained. In all probability they were written by one poet ; the strophe-form of both being the same, and language and rhyme altogether similar.

Of course it is barely possible to give by translation a notion of the musical sound of the original in the case of such a simple lyric ; let the reader fancy it as in the best vein of Tennyson.

— Rosy-colored meadows
To shadows — we see vanish everywhere.
— Wood-birds' warbling dieth,
Sore trieth — them the snow of wintry year.
— Woe, woe ! — what red mouth's glow
Hovers — now o'er the valley ?
Ah, ah ! — the hours of woe !
Lovers it doth rally
No more ; — yet its caress seems cozy.

2

— Ever — her sweet greeting
When meeting — my dear love, stirs wondrous joy.
  — As she walks so airy,
The fairy ! — look, my heart leaps wondrous high !
  Woe, woe ! — what red mouth's glow
    Hovers now o'er the valley?
  Ah, ah ! — the hours of woe !
    Lovers it doth rally
No more ; — yet I shall leave it never.

    — Pleasure — sweet and steady
My lady — scatters with her red mouth's smile,
    And her eyes' sweet beaming
My dreaming — venturous thoughts with bliss beguile.
  — Woe, woe ! — what red mouth's glow
    Hovers now o'er the valley ?
  Ah, ah ! — the hours of woe !
    Lovers it doth rally
No more ; — and I regrets must treasure.

In the following poem by Walther von der Vogelweide, and written in the later period of his life, a peculiar rhythmical novelty is introduced ; and at the
same time a novelty in the construction of the strophe-
form, the usually third part of the strophe being in
this instance placed between the usually first and
second parts. In another poem Walther makes this
third part the first, thus reversing the whole ordinary
order of the strophe. The rhythmical novelty consists in this, that in this usually third part, the epode
of the strophe and antistrophe of the whole verse, the
first word is to be read and sung with a pause before

and after it, so as to make it an isolated line as it were, and the last word of the third part or epode must rhyme with it. These rhythmical constructions were called *pauses*, and were frequently made use of by the later Meistersænger. Now the treatment of pauses, or cæsuras, as Poe calls them, by readers or reciters of poetry, requires, in all cases, great delicacy of ear for rhythm. De Quincey somewhere makes allusion to the peculiar effect of certain Greek iambic lines at their close, and very justly ascribes this effect to a peculiar rendering of the pause. But the pause does not occur only at the end of a line in skillfully written poetry, nor, indeed, always at the end of a line, and what in music the composer indicates completely by signs for pauses, the reader of a poem must often substitute for himself by his own hearing. Shakespeare uses them with most admirable accuracy of hearing. As an example, take the measured stateliness, slow and equal, of rhythm in the Ghost's address to Hamlet, closing : —

"If thou didst ever thy dear father love,"

and Hamlet's heart-breaking outburst, than which nothing could be more exquisitely in place, —

"O God!"

followed by the same regular, slow iambics of the Ghost, and then again broken by an ejaculation.

Here Hamlet's "O God!" is rhythmically and metrically a complete blank verse line, and requires the full time of one, the pause either to fall in it entirely after the "O God!" or partly before and partly after it, as the actor's ear may guide his judgment.

The musical effect of the pauses in these poems appears fully only with the return of the regular metre in the third part of the strophe. The image referred to in the second strophe of this beautiful poem is evidently the poet's body.

THE WORLD'S REWARD.

— May God's grace on my soul alight !
   In this world many a life I've made —
   Both man's and woman's — truly glad ;
Ah, had I but myself put right !
— Cherish — I the body's love, it always grieves my
     soul.
It is a lie, she says, I nourish.
"True — love," she adds, "has different mood and
     stays faithful through all.
Love is both good and true to you."
   — Man, leave the love that leaveth thee,
And to the faithful love thee turn.
That love for which thy heart does burn
   Is nought but foolish vanity.

— A fairsome image was my choice ;
   Woe me, I e'er on it did look,
   Or so much as I did to't spoke :
It has lost beauty both and voice,
— One — wondrous thing did dwell in't ; that has
     flown away.
Since then the image dumb has grown.
Lo ! — its rose-lily color turned so dungeon-gray,
   It lost its perfume and its glow.

—O image, if imprisoned me
Thou holdest, pray my chains unbind !
That we each happier may find ;
  For I must back return to thee.

— World, thy reward I well have seen,
  What thou me giv'st, thou tak'st from me.
  We all have turned our back on thee :
Shame on thee, treating me so mean !
— I — ventured life and soul, 'twas far too much !
    and fame
Full thousand times in thy employ.
Now—am I old, and thou doth hold me as thy game ;
  And if I rage then laughest thou.
  — Aye, laugh thou still a little spell ;
Thy day of sorrow soon will near,
And take from thee what thou took'st here,
  And burn thee in the fires of hell.

It is rather singular, scarcely to be accounted for
by the character of the language of the Minnesinger-
period, as some have attempted to show, that by far
the vast majority of the Minnelieder are composed
in the fundamental rhythm of one to three waltz time,
that is to say, in iambics and trochaics ; dactyls and
anapæsts — the fundamental rhythm of one to two,
galop-time — being of comparatively rare occurrence.
Very few poems, indeed, are composed throughout in
dactyls, though these few include some of the finest,
as, for instance, Ulrich von Lichtenstein's " To the
Beloved," and as a rule, they are introduced only in
the body of iambic or trochaic poems, where peculiar
effects are sought to be introduced.

But it is chiefly the rhythmical construction of the Minnelieder *metres*, that is, of the lines of the strophes, which is worthy of study ; and unless the peculiarity of these constructions is rigidly adhered to in translation, the melodic effect of the *Minnelied* is altogether lost. Most of the previous translations of *Minnelieder* have proved failures on this account. A line of six feet from one of the *Minnelieder* is no more like a line of the same number of feet from Tom Moore, for instance, than a fugue by Bach is like one by some modern Italian. The chief distinction is that, unless particularly so indicated by a cæsura with generally an assonance or rhyme, it is not divided into two parts of three feet each, and that it thus has the real effect of a six feet iambic line ; whereas few modern poems venture to produce the full length, but split it up into shorter metres, thereby depriving themselves utterly of its rhythmic effects. The student of the Minne-poetry is at first quite astonished by the length of lines in the Minnelieder, as well as by the relation of their respective proportions to each other ; lines of six, seven, eight, and nine feet are of quite common occurrence, and in the opposite direction the shortness of lines is equally astonishing, though, of course, the shortness produces no such difficulty in the reading as the long lines often do to the unpracticed eye and ear. At the close of a strophe, for instance, it is not uncommon to have a line of from ten to fifteen feet. These have, of course, to be cut up into parts, and usually the cæsuras are indicated ; but quite often, too, a continued long and uninterrupted sweep of the rhythm is needed to produce the proper effect. Musicians can easily guess how this was readily accomplished by the strain of the melody. The following little Watch-song may serve as a specimen. It is by Winli, one of the sweetest of the Minnesinger, of whose life, however, nothing is known.

— Alas, the woe that smart'st, love !
Now it is day, and thou from me depart'st, love ;
   A loving woman leav'st thou here.

— Ah, well with pity may thy face be tendered ;
No woman her white arms ever surrendered
   To body of a man more dear.

— How shall this end ? alack a day,
Thy manhood and thy courtesy, dear love,
Have under helm and under shield conquered my
     heart with sword and eke with spear, love,
   With hero's hand in bright array.

These Watch-songs, or Day-songs, as they were called, are attempted by almost every one of the Minnesinger ; each one trying to give new form and coloring to the same old Romeo and Juliet theme. The following, by Wolfram von Eschenbach, is one of the best of the kind, and serves to illustrate the art-power of a poet who could neither read nor write : —

— The morning's glance by watcher's song waked,
   spied
   A lady as she hidden
In her dear friend's arms lay cozily.
— Thereof high joys within her bosom died ;
   Her clear eyes unbidden

Tears 'gan wet; she said: "Woe day, ah me!
  — Wild and tame things thee hold dear
And gladly welcome;   I alone not; woe, what shall
      I do?
Now no longer more may stay with me my true,
      Best friend; thy light drives him from here."

— The day with power now through the windows
      broke;
      Much counseled they together;
Unavailing; then great woe broke in on them.
— The loving friend her friend close to her took;
      Her eyes besprinkled either
Pale-grown cheek; her mouth spoke thus her flame:
      — "Twain our hearts, our body one,
All undivided; and our troths do never go apart.
O, great love has so o'errun my loving heart,
      With thee near me, and I with thee!"

— Sadly the man took farewell from his bliss:.
      Their parting love yet moulded
As't came nearer with the day's bright gleams.
— Ah, weeping eyes make sweeter mouth's sweet kiss!
      In last embrace they folded
Their mouths, their breasts, their arms, and their
      white limbs.
      Dared a painter sketch the scene
As they together lay so sweetly, he would enough
      achieve.
Their common love thus cheated still all grief:
      Their love no hate came e'er between.

One of the most beautiful and characteristic of

"Watch-songs" is this one by the Margrave von Hohenburg. It has, moreover, an unusual rhythmical and metrical peculiarity, in the interpolated and repeated warning of the Watchman: "Wake him, Lady!" and the Lady's response: "Sleep, dear fellow!"

— I watch to guard a brave knight's life,
And, beauteous dame, thy name from strife:
    Wake him, Lady!
— God grant, that things chance him so trim,
That he wake up, and none but him!
    Wake him, Lady!
    — No longer wait,
    The time is late;
Nor do I pray alone for his dear sake:
    Wouldst thou him keep,
    Wake him from sleep!
Sleeps he too long the fault is thine, alack!
    Wake him, Lady!

— "Accursèd be thy hateful voice,
Watchman, and thy loud sounding noise!
    Sleep, dear fellow!
— Thy watching was all good enough;
Thy waking 'tis, that hurts my love:
    Sleep, dear fellow!
    — Watchman, I e'er
    Gave thee good cheer,
Cheer that my own heart but too rarely gets.
    Thou dost repay
    By calling day
And banishing sweet joy from my heart's gates:
    Sleep, dear fellow!"

—Thy anger shall me not dismay,
The knight must here no longer stay;
    Wake him, Lady!
— He came to thee, trusting thy faith;
For honor's sake guard thou his path:
    Wake him, Lady!
    — O, Lady dear,
    Should he lose here
His life, then we are also lost with him.
    I sing, I say,
    Now dawns the day.
Wake him, for now my horn *must* break his dream;
    Wake him, Lady!

But it is not alone in the skill wherewith rhyme and
the mechanism of rhythm and metres are handled,
that the Minnesinger unfold wonderful perception
of beauty; the pictures, scenes, thoughts, and descriptions of their poems arouse constantly admiration and delight. Could anything be more sweet
and graceful than the following scene! The poem
is by Johann Hadloub, already mentioned as the
Minnesinger who, under the patronage and direction
of the knights of Manesse, collected all the Minnesongs that could be procured at his time.

— Ah! I saw her sweetly pet a little child,
    And love beguiled
    Straightway my heart.
— She embraced it in her arms right close, and then
    In me, poor man,
    Great grame did start.

—She held up its face with her hands fair and white,
Yea, and pressed it to her mouth and to her cheek;
        And kissed it she
        With sheer delight.

— It did straightway as I also should have done:
        The little one
        Embraced her too.
— It did e'en as if't knew all its happiness;
        Its joy no less
        Seemed full and true.
— Could I then behold it without envy, pray?
Ah, thought I, were I but now that child so free,
        And that she me
        Thus played love's play!

— Then I watched until the child had left her clasp,
        And with fond grasp
        Drew it to me.
—It had seemed so sweet as she had held the dear:
        My heart did stir
        Most blissfully,
— I embraced it closer e'en than she'd held it,
Kissed the sweet, sweet place, where her sweet kiss
        still sat;
        Ah me, how that
        Made my heart beat!

And here is also a lovely one by Christian von Hamle:—

THE MEADOW.

I wish the flow'ry meadow could but utter
    Like yon parrot in the glass,
And tell me how it felt and 'gan to flutter
    When to-day my love did pass,
    And plucked flowers, a glorious mass,
From its field, whilst onward airily flitting
    Her sweet feet trod its grass.

Sir Meadow, since you felt such wondrous pleasure
    Where that time my lady went,
With her white hands gath'ring your flow'ry treasure,
    And gathering, lowly o'er them bent,
    O, Sir Meadow, do consent —
And let me now place my feet where, quitting,
    My love left the grass down-bent.

Sir Meadow, if you but at our next meeting
    Persuade her to relieve my woe,
Her naked feet you often shall feel beating
    Your fields, for there I'll ask her go ;
    Then you'll ne'er be hurt by snow ;
And if she send me a kindly greeting,
    Green like your clover my heart will grow !

Of the following Minnesong by Jacob von Warte,
a knight of an old noble house, Van der Hagen says :
"I still hear in my old age, arising from it the same
sound of the old Minnesong, which it awoke in me
when I first read it in early youth ; it is of uncommon loveliness and sweetness."

— You shall hear songs sweetly pealing
  Everywhere from yonder dale.
— Tuneful songs the spring air filling,
  Over all the nightingale
— Look upon the lawn's broad play
  And upon the glowing heather,
  How her dress she wraps together,
Gayly robed to greet young May.

— Many a kind of flowers peep
  Laughing from the dew of meadows
— Towards the sunshine's glory's sweep:
  O, sweet May-time knows no shadows!
— But this me no hope conveys,
  Since I'm sick with heart-grief's fever:
  She, whom I'd be with forever
Still withholds from me her grace.

— O beloved, noble lady,
  Loose me from my yearning dread!
— Stay my guardian, kind and ready,
  Lest my joys droop sick and dead.
— Needful help I ask of thee,
  If my heart thou lettest go,
  Nothing more can calm my woe:
Sweet, O keep thy grace with me.

— Power on many a one descendeth,
  Thus we hear the wise men saying,
— Yet with mercy's balm not blendeth;
  Thus my lady keeps betraying:
— For me with such power she's chained,
  Without mercy, the beloved!

That my heart-grief unremoved
Must stay with me to the end.

— Love, thou must be ours in common,
  Or of joy my soul stays dead.
Grant that she me sweetly summon
  By her mouth so sweet and red.
— Since thy power me so does stir,
  And thou govern'st all my soul, love,
  As thou choosest — e'en so full, love,
Let thy power grow over her!

A number of felicitous uses of rhymes and rhythm
— the first two parts of each strophe, for instance, being connected by a rhyme of the last word of the first
part with the first of the second — occur in this charming poem by Gottfried von Nifen, one of the most
gracious and lively of the knightly minstrels.   He
seems to have been desperately enamored of a
"red mouth," which also occurs in this as it does indeed in most of his poems.   He was celebrated and
liked at court; of his circumstances we know nothing.

— Hark! I hear the birdlets singing,
  Music through woods sweetly ringing;
Clinging — you see flowers loom through the grass.
  Trace — of early summer-pleasure
  Shows the heather in full measure:
Treasure — of rare flowers and roses red.
  May brings many a blossom glad.
  Had I but my lady's favor,
  Look, with joy I'd glow forever,

Ne'er more sad,
Of many a sorrow free.

— If the blessèd one would grant me
Her love, bliss would soon enchant me,
Haunt me — ne'er should any sorrow move.
— For all solace is but sickly,
She alone can heal me quickly:
Mickly — blessèd woman, comfort now!
— Love, help thou, for time does call.
All — my hopes cling to her dearly:
She can punish me severely.
Why and how
Pray, does she hurt me so?

— O, that her red mouth were willing,
With sweet kiss release revealing,
Healing — my love's wound with its sweet balm!
— Calm — joy, bliss, and honor steady
On my heart would settle ready:
Lady — blessèd woman, comfort now!
Woe that sweet red mouth of thine!
Pine — it made me when its sweetness
Smiled on me first charmèd witness!
These griefs, trow!
Will soon make me look gray.

— Sweetest love, thou work'st great wonder:
Love, from thee I cannot sunder,
Under — thy rule must I henceforth be.
Thee — the sparkling eyes did beckon
Of a woman and have taken,

Shaken — straight into my heart and flown.
— Sweetheart, now be kind and good !
Would — I ever joy draw near me,
You must drive from me — O, hear me,
Blessèd one !
Love's grief — then joy'll be mine.

— Faith, it fitteth not the maiden,
That she keeps me sorrow laden,
Gladden — should she me with ecstasy,
She — meekly loving on me smiling,
All my dreamy grief beguiling,
Toiling — can cure me with love alway.
— Woe, that sweet red mouth of thine !
Pine — my proud mood with love-passion,
Red mouth, made thy sweet expression.
Now quick ! say !
For thou my prayer now know'st.

The following is by Duering, a very sweet and melodious singer : —

LOVE-SONG.

— Alas ! time still does pass from us !
The amorous
Songs of the birds have vanishèd.
The cold and frost make all things dead.
Whither has fled
The bloom of flowers and roses red?
— Where are the dewy meadows and the tree-top's
shady towers ?
Alas! the frost has all destroyed.

There is a void
Of many joys, that erst were ours.

— But me hurts neither frost nor snow,
  For well I know
A laughing mouth — ah me, so sweet !
— It opens like a new-blown rose,
  And redder glows
Than any rose the sun doth greet.
—It is my loved lady's; and could I forget her, pray?
She bringeth happiness most rare ;
  Her body fair
Is my perennial Easter-day.

— Who'er saw such a maid afore?
  To the sea-shore
You'll find none like her, none so fair.
— 'Tis she for whom my heart doth pant.
  Could she relent
And love me, ah, how rich I were !
— Her gladsome eyes would brighten my life with
  love's own glare ;
For her great beauty so beguiles :
  On whom she smiles
Forever is relieved of care.

Nor do the Minnesinger fear weightier themes.
Even so cheerful a poet as Gottfried von Strassburg,
the greatest of that whole age, sings in solemn, ad-
monishing tones, as witness the following of the only
four of his Minnesongs that have been left to us : —

3

ADVICE TO A CHILD.

— Child, if fortune happen to avoid thee,
And God give thee poverty — of body and of riches,
— Thou must learn in patience to abide thee,
And must not nurse grief thereat — in thought or in
    thy speeches.
— Thou should'st thank the Lord for it — with heart
    and soul forever;
And to drive it from thy mind endeavor;
Look, then t'will be told of thee in heaven to thy
    favor.

— Child, this poverty, know, dearest fellow
Bear it with a willing mind — believe me, 'tis the better
— And your soul in hell's pool shall not wallow.
Body and soul can both be thus — be ridden from
    sin's fetter.
— Poverty against God's wrath — the highest savior
    proveth.
Between God and us such love it moveth
As no angel e'en can move: — this thee to think be-
    hooveth.

— Child, this poverty by Him was courted
Who was highest, yea and first — and shall be without
    ending;
— Poverty at his birth-place consorted,
Where his sweet maid-mother lay — him into life's
    grief sending.
— Poverty his night and day; — in poverty life leav-
    ing;

And in poverty our grace achieving :
Poverty be too thy choice from hell thy soul retrieving.

— Child, let no man e'er on this deceive thee :
Unless thou hast poverty — through God in thy heart
    nursed,
— From the path to hell nought can relieve thee,
Where thou'lt suffer without end — the torments of
    th' accursèd.
— God his mother would not e'en — give two king-
    doms of heaven.
Harshest poverty her here was given,
Whom in worth her equal was — no man or angel
    even.

— Child, God with his own mouth thus has spoken :
That the heavenly kingdom, none — but the willing
    poor inherit.
— Cherish in thy heart this as a token,
— And let not the lust for wealth — succeed e'er to
    enter it.
— Wealth is of unmeasured harm — unto the soul's
    salvation.
For it leads to sin through sore temptation :
O, from it thy mind turn quick — thou'lt gain the
    heavenly station.

— Dearest child, I now will tell thee fully
Wherefore wealth brings so much harm — when 'tis
    not used in measure :
— It makes men court seldom God, the Holy,
It has many and many a soul — turned from his
    grace's treasure.

— It gives birth to vain conceit — and to God's will
  forgetting.
It craves women, wine, and sweetened eating;
Whereof many a one thou seest — hell's downward
  pathway beating.

— Child, now I will tell thee more, declaring
Wherefore wealth brings so much harm — to God,
  and works man's damage.
— It makes many a fool so overbearing
That his puffed-up heart no more — to any one shows
  homage.
— Moreover, 'tis of such a kind — that he, to whom't
  grows dearer,
Straightway spurns humility, sweet cheerer,
And thereby from God estranged — to hell draws
  steadily nearer.

— Child, now I to thee'll unfold, moreover,
Wherefore wealth brings so much — harm to things
  divine, and grievance.
— It can with great grame the soul's life cover,
It can bring thee sore distress — from which there's
  no retrievance.
— It from out thy heart God's love — and its sweet-
  ness expelleth.
"Where thy hoard is, there thy heart eke dwelleth!"
God himself said; and this word — to thee 'tis that
  He't telleth.

— Child, now I will prove to thee still clearer,
Wherefore wealth brings so much harm — to th'
  angel's host in heaven.

— Look, it maketh many an old man serer,
That in good works he doth grow — quite dumb and
    foolish even.
— Then his lustful heart the love — of wealth so
    tightly clenches :
God from out his very heart he wrenches,
God, who saved him on the cross — with his heart's
    blood rare trenches.

— Child, if thee the people scorn and slander,
That thou hast not mickle wealth — do not become
    defected ;
— God will pour on thee his love, so tender,
In that hour when the mere rich — shall be by Him
    rejected.
— Choose thou either here thy weal — and there woe
    without ending,
Or choose here thy woe, and courage lending
There thy everlasting weal — where sorrow has no
    standing.

— Child, God surely nought so dearly rateth
As He doth humility — in men and like in women.
— On the other hand He nought so hateth
As conceit and pride, for they — are doomed t'obey
    hell's summon.
— Now these find'st thou nowhere more — than midst
    those that are wealthy,
Who may follow them or bold or stealthy,
Night or day ; but for thy soul, — dear child, they are
    not healthy.

— Child, to five things bear thou love the dearest,
If thy poverty thou want'st — God ever to reward
 thee.
— *Purity* keep unto thee the nearest,
Chastity put in thy heart; with — *Mildness* thy soul
 guard thee.
— Night and day *Humility* — keep into thy mind
 sowing,
Towards man and woman *Patience* showing:
Look, thus shalt thou never more — be with the
 damned found going.

— When the wealthy do at last draw nigher
To old age, that they no more — their pride display
 can stately,
— They the flames of pride in·youth fan higher,
And teach them t'indulge conceit — whereat God
 sorrows greatly.
Thus their pride they nourish, till — to death at last
 they passing
Try t'accept for what there's no redressing:
God us all through his Son's death — send us grace
 and blessing!

In this, again, enthusiastic Mulnhusen chants the
wondrous beauty of —

MY LADY.

— She has a body fair as light,
 She has crisp hair, yellow and curled.
— She has a throat as snow so white;
 No finer woman holds this world.

—I'd rather be with her than be even with God in
  paradise :
 Lord, in her love make thou me wise !
 — The sun did ne'er so bright appear,
  But my love still more beauty brought.
 — Her eyes stand open, bright, and clear ;
  God making her, forgot e'en nought.
—I would not take the crown of Rome, were't offered
  for her body me ;
 She pleases me so mightily.

 The next one, by Ulrich von Wintersteten, a noble
knight, has a peculiarity which deserves attention, in
that the refrain is not a part of the strophe itself, but
is hung on as an appendix to the three parts of each
stanza.

WHERE THY HEART IS, THERE IS EKE THY HOARD.

 — Summer its great glory watches,
  For this is its time !
 — Let the poet look, he catches
  All there is sublime
 — In the forest and the grass-decked lea.
   The fair vestures
   Of the pastures
   He may see ;
 And how flowers with green fields agree.
  It is an old, old spoken word :
  Where thy heart is, there is eke thy hoard.

 —I at last have now discovered
  A most glorious hoard,

— There my soul has e'er since hovered
    Without further word,
— By that hoard, from which but pain has grown.
      For the pure one
      So demure, on
      Me looks down !
Yet she is my heart's love, she alone.
    It is an old, old spoken word :
    Where thy heart is, there is eke thy hoard.

— My hoard must be virtues hoarding,
    And a highflown mood.
— For the hoard that I am guarding
    Is a woman good.
— In her thorough goodness so like gold :
      Her behavior
      Hath a flavor
      As if old,
For her virtues shine most manifold.
    It is an old, old spoken word :
    Where thy heart is, there is eke thy hoard.

— Many a one, his hoard concealing,
    From it joy receives.
— But mine stirs but angry feeling
    And mere scoldings gives.
— Thus my dearest hoard to me doth show
      Useless every way.
      But Love's gay
      Cupido
Hit my heart, so it stays full of woe.
    It is an old, old spoken word :
    Where thy heart is, there is eke thy hoard.

— Love, ah, 'tis the strongest craving
    Of all earthly things,
— On the earth there is no saving
    From the wounds love brings.
—Wisdom, hoard, they both bow down to thee,
        Now bliss ; sorrow
        When to-morrow
        Yearning 's free :
O, force thou, Love, my hoard, e'en as thou hast
    forced me.
    It is an old, old spoken word :
    Where thy heart is, there is eke thy hoard.

The bloom of the Minnesong passed away gradually in the latter half of the thirteenth century, when its freshness and life of rhythmical form and compact completeness of stanza gave way to the pure mechanism of construction which a new school of singers brought into play. The knights forsook the art and left it to the citizens, upon whom the passion of poetizing now seemed to have seized. But the citizen did his work citizen-like, and not in the enthusiastic way of the knight. The Minne-poem became more and more didactic, theologic, and politic in content ; more and more forced in form. The strophes began to assume extraordinary length, so that the ear could no longer gather the musical relation of its various parts ; the lines, also, either inordinately drawn out or unmusically short ; the rhythm stiff and unwieldy. The poems evinced lack of clearness and precision ; unwieldiness of speech ; search after quaint, new similes drawn from unknown fables, doctrines, historical data, etc. ; mystery bordering on downright nonsense; assumption of profound thoughtfulness to hide emptiness ; in short, all the symptoms which characterize the modern Browning-school, and which characterize, indeed, every school of merely artificial art.

Of course the change was gradual ; and partly also probably influenced by so many of the Minnesinger leaving the freer life of Southern Germany for that of the northern parts, as far up, indeed, as Denmark, where in King Eric VI. they found a patron devoted and liberal, like their own Herrmann of Thüringen. But the didactic element prevailed in those northern parts, where a whole host of Minnesinger now began to spring up and put Puritanism and political party spirit into the lovely form of the Minnesong and Lay. Hermann Damen, Meisner, Sonnenburg, and Rumeland are amongst the most noted of these. Wizlav IV., Prince of Rügen, and the last of known princely singers, also belonged to this northern tribe, and sang of theology, though, it must be admitted, as a true prince, likewise of love.

Above these tower Conrad von Wurzburg, who lived toward the last years of the thirteenth century, and is to be ranked amongst the very foremost of Minnesinger, wonderfully pure and sweet in his rhymes, graceful in rhythm, happy and easy in the subjects of his poems, and besides the author of many short narrative poems as well as of a magnificent song to the Virgin entitled " The Golden Smithy " ; and Regenbogen, who left his profession of a smith from an irresistible attraction to forge poetry, and succeeded in no way badly.

But chief of all of this later school ranks Regenbogen's rival, Heinrich von Meissen, better known by the name Frauenlob, an appellation given him because in a prolonged controversy with Regenbogen he maintained the supremacy of the word "Frau," Lady, over that of "Weib," Woman. It had become quite customary for the new citizen poets to assume such nicknames, and many of them are known to us only by them. In this poetical contest of Frauenlob's, almost all the poets of that time took part. Walther von der Vogelweide gave his vote thus : —

WOMAN AND LADY.

— "Woman" must ever be a woman's highest name,
And honors more than " Lady," if I know right.
— Now if there's one who holds her womanhood in
  shame,
Let her attend these verses and choose now right.
  — 'Mongst the ladies some are bad,
  'Mongst the women such are rare ;
  Woman's name and love have had
  Pleasant sound, faith everywhere.
  And whate'er may ladies mar :
  All the women ladies are.
  Doubtful praise man scorneth,
As oft that of " a Lady"; but " Woman " is a praise
  that all adorneth.

But Frauenlob deserves his high rank among the
poets of this later school of Minnesinger chiefly by
the marvelous ease and power with which he controls

all the artifices of his craft, under which his fellow-poets so often succumb into laborsome prose. He is the very Swinburne of his age: serene ruler of all the tricks of rhythm, rhyme, and alliteration. Take the following lines from his magnificent Minne-Lay as a proof: —

> " Wer kan — werden man
> Vueren up der eren plan
> *Mit gewelvet pfellel varwes mundes kusses bieten ?* "

As illustrations of the manner in which this later school did their work, we give a poem on the Trinity by Meisner, and a stanza from each of the three famous poems written by Frauenlob, Regenbogen, and Marner in their " Song Tone." Concerning these Song Tones, it will be necessary to state that when the still later school of Meistersænger came into existence, after the total expiration of the Minnesinger-period, and after the knightly life of chivalry had been supplanted by the burgher life of citizenhood, it made no attempts even to rival either the inventive skill of the first Minnesinger, or the mechanical art construction of the later ones. They contented themselves with imitation ; and as the mechanical poetry tickled their admiration more, on the whole, and was in truth the only one possible to imitate, the school of the Meistersænger fell upon the inherited schemes of metres and stanzas of the later Minnesinger, and upon the basis of these, constructed their own unfathomably tedious poems. These schemes or tones received each a peculiar name. Thus there were long tones, new tones, golden tones, over-golden tones, etc. To construct readily a poem on such a given scheme certainly required great skill, practice, and knowledge of language; but with these accomplishments any one could also make a poem, whether he possessed other poetical gifts or not. The Meistersænger, having formed a guild of poets, into which no one could be admitted till after severe examination into his mastery over various tones, etc., they chose from out of all inherited tones four, which were then called the crowned tones, and every candidate for admission had to compose a poem in the metre and music of these four tones before he was crowned as master poet. The four crowned tones thus selected were the long tones of Marner, Regenbogen, Frauenlob, and Mügglin. Mügglin, as not belonging to this period, we leave out; of Frau-enlob and Regenbogen we have already spoken; Marner was one of the most learned poets of his time, and also became one of the most popular, on account of a very long theological poem written in the same celebrated long tone.

THE TRINITY.

I.

— I marvel how above me the clouds fly night and
      day;
I marvel where the night stays during day, and where
      the day goeth at night
    Whose light to-day us shone.
— I marvel at the many marvels of God's display;
I marvel how the sun takes from the moon whenever
      morning breaks her light;
    And how three Gods are one.

— Without beginning, without end, one God ;
The one I triple, people, and make my abode ;
The Trinity thus tripled in three names holdeth
    sway ;
The three, one God within one Godhead, Holy Ghost,
    God Father, Jesus, stay ;
    Almighty God for aye !

II.

— Above all wonders of the world remark a mickle
    wonder ;
How soul and flesh one body are,
And how the soul 's a spirit, and how it lives forever.
— And how God's word is man and Christ, Christ
    God's child here and yonder ;
    God's three names, too, do thou declare ;
Father, Son, and Holy Ghost ; three names that none
    can sever.
    — See how God one in one doth flow,
    And cunningly doth render
    The one in two ; say yea, not no,
    If thou wouldst life engender ;
    Part one in three, three in one show,
Tripled and joined if thou thee wouldst unto Christ
    surrender.

STANZA IN REGENBOGEN'S SONG FROM HIS
HYMN TO THE VIRGIN.

— How spake Isaiah in the dearth?
" Ye heavens, bend down to earth, and clouds pour
    forth your waters !

> Earth, ope thou thy wounds most wide,
> And bring to us a God with power of saving!"

> — Maria, Virgin, thou'rt the earth:
> Thou'rt blessed, O wife and mother 'bove all earth's
>   blessed daughters.
> God's Son oped thy heart, sweet bride;
> Then came the dew the prophet erst was craving;

> — And likewise in her breast the sword,
> When from the Holy Spirit she received
>   The heavenly, the quickening word,
> And the new wondrous mystery perceived.
>   Maria! Thou the earth, I wot,
>   Art of Isaiah's word:
> Thou bringest us the true Christ Jesus, Lord.
> Ye dews and ye sweet rains from heaven,
> And clouds, bore then the Holy Spirit down,
>   By the blest word to Gabriel given,
>   Who then from heaven brought down her crown.
> O, blessèd dew of earth and heaven forever blooms
>   what you to bloom restored.
>   O Jew, damnation is thy lot
> That thy belief with ours does not accord.

STANZA IN FRAUENLOB'S LONG TONE FROM HIS HYMN TO THE VIRGIN.

> — Maria, God's own Mother, Daughter, Bride most
>   sweet,
>   Let me repeat
>   To thee the angel's greeting,
>   When thou God cam'st meeting,

Then taking Him into thy life ; also thy repeating:
"I am the handmaid of the Lord; his will be done
      unto me."

— O Lady, let me linger on the grace so rare,
    When thou didst bare
    To Simeon's sword thy tender
    Breast in the temple's splendor.
Let me recall his sufferings too, the life He did
    surrender,
Mother, before thy very eyes, thy lifeless heart; ah,
    woe me!

— Life hallowed in all thoughts of mine.
Let me recall the grace divine
    Of that Child thine ;
    Thy joy benign,
When his ascension saw thine eyen;
And God the same did thee assign ;
Thou, source of all man's blessedness, O, from all
    sin renew me !

STANZA IN MARNER'S LONG TONE FROM HIS HYMN TO THE VIRGIN.

Maria, blooming almond-tree,
    The heavenly manna's shrine,
From sin's grim death-frost set us free,
    For thou art helper all divine :
Thou the royal glorious throne of the wise king Solo-
    mon.

Thou Judith, who mad'st valiantly
    The prize of victory thine;
Thou Esther, queen by king's decree,
    Who, when in need thy people pine,
Dar'st interpose thy pleading tone, and front the
    death-doom for thine own.

Thou, pure Jael, now hast slain Sisera, haughty king;
Thou art she who from the serpent took his venomed
    sting:
    Thou glorious pilot-star!
Thou art the wise wife Abigail; and sinners thee ap-
    proach from far.
Thou wert beloved by David, king, who slew proud
    Goliath,
    (Craftily, in faith!)
    And cleft his head in wrath,
    Whence wisdom smoothed e'er his path.
O Mother, pure and chaste, sweet Maid, turn from us
    sin's hateful breath,
So that we gladly thee may worship, and thy great
    honor ever own!

While the Minnesong thus on the one hand was
frozen into pure mechanical versifying, it on the other
hand and from another school received, if possible, a
still greater injury by being dragged down into the
region of vulgarity and obscenity. Nithart, though
certainly one of the most gifted of the Minnesinger,
was the chief leader in this downward movement, and
the vast number of his songs transmitted to us to
substantiate, as it were, his popularity, turn chiefly

4

upon vulgar descriptions of village brawls, and amorous dialogues. His great genius and illimitable command over language appear chiefly in his Lays. He was indeed the knight-minstrel turned into the minstrel-vagabond and tavern-house loafer. Songs that would characterize his peculiar *genre*, it would be almost impossible to give. The following two show him in his better mood : —

FAREWELL TO THE WORLD.

— All that in the Summer full of glory was,
Now begins to sorrow at the Winter's long and heavy
    time,
And the birdlets' warblings now have vanished every-
    where.
— Altogether perished are the flowers and grass,
And behold how cold and grim snow-coverings o'er
    the forests climb ;
Whilst the meadow and the heath are stretched out
    waste and bare.
    — Hence I raise this lamentation :
    I no more enjoy me,
    And I fear this tribulation
    Never will pass by me.

— Perhaps you may wonder what my plaint can
    be,
Which I in repentant spirit did unto my friends dis-
    close.
I will tell you, and you shall acknowledge't must be
    truth ;

— Alas, never is a man of sins here free,
And, moreo'er, the longer't stays the worse in Chris-
    tendom it grows.
This reflection darks my days and kills off all
    my youth.
        — Shall I then to joys resign me
          My heart does not cherish?
        And not rather round Him twine me
          Who'll not let me perish?

— If I, sinner, try to bathe me in repentance,
Then my lady asks me quick to sing a song unto
    her child;
Do I then try to withdraw me from her urging e'er,
    — She does threaten me to cut off my acquaintance.
Her immodesty has thus fore'er my thoughts from
    her beguiled;
I am in that mood wherein my soul from sin I'd clear,
        — Which I from God have led astray
          By my voluptuous measures;
        God's angel must guide me the way
          To heaven's soothing treasures.

— Woman without honor, what wouldst have of me?
Thousand young ones ready are hereafter to stand in
    my place;
I'm resolved to serve a Lord, who me for Him has
    won.
    — From this time I will no more your singer be.
Woe me that I ever did myself unto your court
    abase?
This my soul's salvation has for a long time undone.

— That I did not fly from you
Makes my sorrow greater,
And to God my soul withdrew,
Whose reward is better.

— My lady, she is older than a thousand years,
And still is stupider than is a little ungrown seven-
years child.
So weak-minded unto me was ne'er a woman
known, —
— She has ever led me stray; and I have fears
She hopes still I may by her again be captured and
beguiled, —
For this to a messenger, sent by me, she did own.
— She made offer openly
Of her great affection.
But I replied: Away with thee!
And prompt me no defection.

— Now since the wise are always God's own chil-
dren named,
Could I be wise I also should be one of his own chil-
dren's choir;
But their abode, alas! too far removed is from me,
— For all the fools by love of world are ever
claimed.
O Lord of heav'n! guide thou me, and my soul with
Thy great love inspire!
Strength above all the Christians I, God, hope to gain
from Thee.
— Thus I my soul's salvation may,
O Lord, from Thee recover!

And evermore in thy sweet way
Remain thy pray'rful lover.

SPRING–SONG.

— The wood that looked so grisly
— With snow and ice lifelessly,
— Is now with glorious colors blest.
  O, children, haste
  T'enjoy its treat,
And where gay flowers grow swing your feet.

— On many a *green* branch swinging,
— Little birdlets singing
— Warble sweet notes in the air.
  Flowers fair
  There I found
Green spread the meadow all around.

— I am a friend of Maytime,
— 'Twas then I saw in daytime
My love dance in the linden's shade ;
  The leaves all play'd
  To turn away
From her the heat of the sunny day.

A Dance-song by Tanhuser must conclude this
selection of Minnesongs ; it illustrates moreover the
Nithart style of Minnelied, just alluded to. Whether
this knight-poet Tanhuser is the prototype of the
legendary Tannhäuser of the Venus-mountain, is un-
certain ; though his poems are vividly amorous enough

to justify the suspicion. Most of those poems are in the form of lays. Tanhuser was a much admired poet of his time, and this Dance-song of his is certainly an admirable production, calling up the scenes of the village dance with dramatic truthfulness.

DANCE–SONG.

— In Christmas times so cheery
We should remove all thoughts that make us dreary.
　　Too long we've lived in dolor ;
Now follow me, for I your hearts will cheer ye.
　　— I'll sing for you some dances.
Look! on your flower-crowned fair one cast your
　　glances,
　　Her cheeks of rosy color —
Ah, how your hearts would laugh if they were near ye !
　　— Whensoe'er the fairest
Bends forward, rapture thrills me, O the rarest !
　　And her bosom's sinking
Keepeth my mind on love forever thinking.

— She is so sweet, so pretty,
I'll sing her praise in my readiest ditty :
　　Her hands so shapely standing,
Her fingers as queen's tapering so slowly, —
　　— Thus is she formed and shapen.
Moreo'er so well timed all her speeches happen,
　　Without false praises spending,
I well may say she looks an empress wholly ;
　　— Aye, I do pledge my favor
With all of you, that in this land I never

Beheld so fair a creature :
Perfect in form and pure in every feature.

    — Aye, dance away and clatter,
So you no dust upon my fair one scatter.
    Look not at her often,
For if you do I fear you'll lose your senses.
    — Her laugh so beguiling —
Ah, thousand hearts must break when she is smiling.
    Her moist glances soften,
And in my heart awaken love's sweet trances.
    — Stand back, ye boys and lasses !
Make for the fairest room whene'er she passes.
    This is but your duty :
I hold no other land holds such a beauty.

    — Ah, laugh now at my folly :
I tremble when her toes peep out so jolly,
    They are so shapely standing !
Ah comely form and dear belovèd sweetheart !
    — Dance, my love ! ye follow !
O ne'er were feet so rounded, small and hollow.
    If thee please not their ending
Know thou, my friend, that thou no judge of feet art.
    — White are her legs and curvèd ;
Her curled hair's waves have made me all unnervèd ;
    Her shape perfectly moulded !
All women ought to be in her is well unfolded.

    — Thou dearly loved, good creature,
Move here, stand there, perfect in ev'ry feature !

No beauty like't in story :
Thy mouth so red, thy eyen so sweetly calling,
     — Thy cheeks, that glow so rosy !
White thy throat, its necklace there so cozy,
     Thou dear summer glory !
Thy hair as full as I could wish it falling.
     — Thy breasts, so sweetly heaving, —
Dance, love, O, dance, love sweet past all believing !
     Let thy gentle glances
Linger on me, sweet love, and stir my senses !

CHAPTER II.

THE MINNELAY.

THE Minnelay is distinguished from the Minnesong in this, that it lacks the triplicity of
the strophe-form and the sameness of the
strophes. Hence the strophe itself in its own construction is completely independent, and each strophe
of a Lay is again also completely independent in regard
to the others. At least, so far as known, there was no
regular law on this matter. From the descriptions
given by Lichtenstein and Gottfried von Strassburg,
as well as from the form of the Lay itself, it would appear as if its singing had usually required a quicker
time movement and more violent modulations and musical transitions from low to high notes than the common song. At any rate, being invariably rendered with
the accompaniment of some stringed instrument, the
music was a necessary element for the perception of
its full rhythmical beauty. Not a very large number
of Lays have been preserved. Most of these have
for their subject the general one of all Minne-poetry :
love, the seasons, and the state of society. Several
Lays of Tanhuser also bring in matters of geograph-
ical and historical lore in an odd, comical way, whilst
Nithart shows his power over language, wherein he
is excelled only by the great German humorist of

the sixteenth century, Johann Fischart, nowhere so astonishingly and with such felicitous effect as in his Lays. In a number of the Lays the last line recounts the breaking of the fiddle-bow or strings, whereby both the singing of the Lay and the dance, which it generally excited, were put to an end. Ulrich von Lichtenstein has some excellent Lays, but we here give two by the good knight Ulrich von Wintersteten, who seems to have had a preference for this form of Minne-poetry. Of the poet's life little or nothing is known except that he lived about in the very bloom of Minne-poetry, under the Emperor Frederick II. Both of these Lays seem to be somewhat connected; and an exact metrical correspondence appears also between the several strophes; for instance, between strophes 1, 2, 3, 4, and strophes 9, 10, 11, 12; also between the 5th and 6th, the 7th and the 8th, and the 13th and 14th in the first Lay. In the second Lay the 1st and 2d, and the 3d and 4th, and the 5th and 6th strophes have identical rhythmical arrangements.

A LAY.

1.

Ah, love, mark how thy glances
Awake
And shake
My senses
With sweet love trances ;
And yet how full joy still mischances.

2.

Fool I, I borrow
Sorrow
Forever ;
Sever
From me all gladness and pleasure,
Love, keep sending,
Kindly lending,
Befriending
Help to my heart without measure.

3.

If with the dear, I — believe me ! —
Could dally
And rally
From grief me :
Sorrow would have to leave me
And joy come at once and reprieve me.

4.

Since I 'gan singing
Unclinging
Seems weariness.
Yet dreariness
Follows me every hour.
Love, do thou smiling,
Grim grame beguiling,
Joy on me shower.

5.

How shall I joy now recover ?
In me

Through thee
It finds no clover.
Thou must unbind, love, thy lover,
Thou must, or make gladness come over.

6.

Give me but once, sweet savior,
One sigh!
Since I
Of thy behavior
Sing songs of the rarest blown flavor,
Ease heart grief by granting sweet favor!

7.

A pretty
Ditty
Gladly I'll wake, love!
Take, love,
My song, thou so lovely and witty.

8.

Ease me,
Release me,
Quick from my fetters,
Begetters
Of grief, that yet never gave peace me!

9.

Sweet one, let me not languish!
Quiet
The riot
Of my great anguish!
Let love me not *vanquish!*
Protect me, O love, from that anguish!

10.

Shall me thy sweetness turn sour?
My mood
Doth brood
On love's wondrous power, —
I tremble and cower
With fear, love, my heart may devour.

11.

Ah, how scatter,
Shatter
Sorrow?
Borrow,
Sweet love, relief for my sadness.
Thy looks, lady,
Thrills my steady
Heart too ready:
For never arouse they fond gladness.

12.

Alas and woe me!
For unto me
Cometh grief now.
Relief now
Can come but from love's addresses.
Lady, weep thou;
For me keep thou,
Heap thou
On me thy caresses!

13.

Dear lovèd one,
Pure, sweet one, meet me!

Blessèd, my own,
By thy great goodness, greet me!

14.

Yea, I am dead
If love doth not come to me;
It were too bad,
If love should thus undo me.

ANOTHER LAY.

1.

Look me dearest,
Nearest!
Fearest
Man's scoff thou?
Rose of the valley,
Dally!
Rally
And laugh thou!

2.

Let all heart-aching,
Soul-breaking,
Forsaking
Soon leave me!
Let me succeed, love!
Speed, love!
Take heed, love,
To grieve me.

3.

Blessedness thy red mouth showers ;
Could I kiss it thousand hours,
Ah me !
Gone were all my yearning grame ;
Now all dead of joy I am ;
Ah me !

4.

Rich of virtue, sweet and best,
Let me see, thou pity hast
On me.
I should ever grameless stay
If one look on me would stray
From thee !

5.

Lady, now to me do so
That great joy on me may flow,
Thou virtue's choicest flower !
If thou wilt, fore'er must go
From my heart all grame and woe,
And bliss must on me shower.

6.

Ah, sweetest love, come loving be,
To love resign thee lovingly,
That I no more be worried,
And sigh no more for thy sweet sake,
My yearning heart, else love, wilt break,
And in its grief be buried.

But it was not alone on the field of the general
Minnesong-subjects that the Lay unfolded its infinite

capacity of form to best advantage. Even as in modern music the regular symphony form is generally abandoned for that of the "symphonic poem," and as in modern poetry the regular strophe-form of song has been generally abandoned for the irregular ; take, for instance, Poe's "Bells," or Tennyson's "Lotus-eaters" as examples of such irregular songs or lays — on account of its greater capacity in some instances to open up wondrous rhythmical beauties, and partly also, it must be confessed, because it is more easy to compose and write beautifully in an irregular than in a regular form, — so the Minne-poets soon transferred the Lay to other regions. As a legitimate subject of the general Minnesong, it had celebrated from the first the glory of the Virgin, and one of the very best of all Lays is the following one by Walther von der Vogelweide, which has this theme : —

LAY TO THE VIRGIN.

God, Thy Threehood, which yonder
Thou from the first didst ponder,
We here confess a wonder :
Tripling't in Thy dread presence :
The Threehood is one essence.

One God, mighty Creator !
Thy power its self-begetter,
Can grow nor less nor greater.
O, send thy Word's sweet fetter !
Us led astray that hater —
By sin's alluring kisses, —
The prince of hell's abysses.

— His guile and our weak flesh, ah we!
Have sore estranged us, Lord, from Thee,
And since these two powers are so bold,
Whilst Thou both in Thy strength dost hold,
O Lord, for Thy own glory's sake,
Help us their fearful chains to break.
Yea, let thy blessèd strength secure
And fill us with such power t'endure.

As must increase Thy praises
And spread Thy glory's phases:
This him vexation raises,
Who taught us sin's disgraces,

And who t'unchasteness us has fettered,
His strength will by Thy strength be shattered,
Thereof Thy praises shall wide be scattered,
And that pure maid's, untouched by hatred,
Who down on us salvation flattered
By her sweet son, and grace us gathered.

Behold, O maid and mother, — how Christendom lies
    wan!
Thou blooming rod of Aaron — uprising morning
    dawn!
Ezekiel's gate that never — was opened, as 'tis said,
Through which the King of Glory, — came in and
    out, sweet maid!
E'en as the sunshine passes — through the unstainèd
    glass,
Thus birth did give to Christ the pure — who maid
    and mother was.

5

A bush fire caught — yet never aught — of it the
    living flame there ate,
All fresh and green — remained its sheen —
    unscorched it passed its fiery fate,
Such the thronely — Maid, the only — maid who
    in a virgin state

    — Was e'er maid mother of a child
    Without being by man defiled;
    And 'gainst all human wit and word
        The true Christ Lord
    Bore, who from sin has won us.
    — Hail us that she birth given hath
    Him, who our death hath slain to death,
    Who with his blood did make the bath,
        That cleansed the wrath
    Eve's guilt had put upon us.

For the throne of — Solomon, thou, — Lady, art a tem-
    ple
rare, and thou the fit commander !
Balm-tree blowing — pearl rare glowing — o'er all
    maidens art thou, maid, a maid of queenly splen-
    dor !
God's nurse cheery — thy womb, Mary, — a palace was,
    that held inclosed the lamb so pure and tender !

    — The lamb doth hold
    Each of his fold
    Alike true gold.
    They him behold
    And turn whene'er he turneth.

— This lamb Christ is,
True God, O bliss!
And ne'er remiss
To make thee his ;
He thy least move discerneth.

O pray to Him, that He, true friend,
Whate'er our need requires may send,
And comfort from above us lend :
His praise the brighter burneth.

— Thou maid of passing pleasure !
Thou'rt like in every measure,
To Gideon's fleece — rare treasures !
Which God with his sweet dew of heaven bespeckled
— A word, o'er all words ventured,
The gates of thy ears entered,
Whose sweetness since has centered,
And in and through thee, Queen of Heaven, has
trickled.

— That which has from the word upgrown,
Now free from childish ways is shown :
It grew from words and became a man,
Now mark and all the wonders scan :
A God, who'd always been God, grew
To be a man and man's ways show !
— All wonders, that he ever had
Achieved, by this he outwondrèd,
This same great wonder-doer's home
Was but a modest maiden's womb,
Full forty weeks, no more nor less,
Without the least sin or distress.

—Now pray we to the mother
And to the mother's bairn,
One pure, and good the other,
Harm from our souls to turn.
— For without them none ever
May here or there be cured.
Who doubts their passing favor
Is foolishly assured.

How can that man be savèd there,
Who, of his evil deeds aware,
Does not rouse heart's-repentance rare,
Since God forgiveness granteth ne'er

But unto those who at all hours
Deep in their hearts arouse remorse,
'Tis well known to us all: no force
Cured ever soul from the dread sores
The sword of sin left in their cores,
Unless repentance ope'd their pores.

But rare is our repenting:
O God, keep Thou us haunting
With thy love-fire enchanting!
Thy Spirit, grace us granting,

Can hardest hearts make tender
And give a new life's splendor:
All should to it surrender.

Where He remorse doth moving know,
There He remorse doth cause to grow:

The wildest heart He so hath tamed,
That of all sin it grew ashamed.

— Now send us, Father, Thou and Son — that same
spirit unto us!
With its sweet dew it shall refresh — and our parched
hearts o'er flow us,
— Alas! unchristian things have filled — all Christendom o'er full:
Where Christendom lies sickly thus — it grieveth
ev'ry soul.

It thirsteth for the — doctrine's love, the — words that
used to come from Rome.
If Rome kept pouring — it, aye, and storing — as for-
merly
      soon cure would come.

      — All the grief it ever bore,
Came from Simony's dread sore;
Now of friends it is so poor,
      It dare no more
Prefer complaint or grumble.
— Christendom and Christenhood,
He, who fitted both so good,
Equally long, equally broad,
      Both love and load,
Willed also we should humble

— In Christ as Christians live in union.
And since He built up this communion,
      We should not now it sever.

— The Christian, who speaks Christenhood
With words, but not in works of good,
   Stays half a heathen ever.
— We words and works equally need;
One is without the other dead;
   God, steer us to both's favor!

     — And lend us aid!
     For Thou hast laid
     What Thy hand made,
  To man's mind kindly patent.
— Now soften, Lady, us this scorn,
Mother of mercy, chosen born,
Thou stingless rose without a thorn,
  Thou sunlight never latent!

Thy praises raise the angel's choir.
Yet raised they ne'er so high its spire,
But its completion may reach higher,

  However much was sung
  By voices and by tongue
  All orders of things among
  On earth e'en as in heaven.
  This we remind thee even,

And for our sins do pray to thee,
That thou would'st hear us graciously,
And ring thy pray'r, heav'n-filling,
To Mercy's fountain pealing,
Sweet hope in us revealing
Our sins may yet be healing,

Wherewith we grievously are laden.
Help us to wash these off, sweet maiden,

With earnest, true repentance — for they oppress us
    sore,
And without God and without thee — they'll leave
    us never more.

But the fullest force of the Lay-form is illustrated
by Frauenlob in his version of Solomon's Song, a version that was universally celebrated at his time and
has since again become an object of earnest admiration to the present German generation. Its argument
is, in brief, this : —

Taking the maiden of Solomon's Song in her accepted theological significance as the bride, daughter,
and mother of the triune God, this wondrously musical lay gathers images of nature, fable, history, and
mythology to celebrate her glory. From strophes of
the simplest construction it rises, gradually increasing the volume of both lines and strophes, to strophes
of forty-six lines, interrupted only once by a strophe,
so musical, that even the eye can hear it : —

> — Wie die doene
> Schoene — loene
> Schenken uz der armonîen ;
> Wie sich modeln drîes drîen ;
> Wie die stcige, velle schrîen,
> Mak man hoeren
> In niun koeren:
> Den schal nieman mak zerstoeren,

Da min vriedel der vil schoene schaffet unser beider
    dink.
                    — Balde vroene,
            Troene, — kroene
    Mir ein kuessen, sun den gerten ;
    Miner menschleit schiltgeverten,
    Mit dem kuenge Jesse zerten ;
            Snoze im troume
            Nam er min goume ;
            Under einem apfelboume
Wart erwecket ich so suezlich ; seht, daz tet der jun-
    gelink.
                    Evovae!

The musical charm of this magnificent poem is extraordinary, and in allowing it to work its full sensuous effect, one can imagine how this poet was able to
excite the admiration of his contemporaries to such a
degree, that at his death ladies carried his body to
the grave with great weeping and lamentations, and
upon his grave so great a quantity of wine was poured
that it ran all around the church.   In the words of
Albert of Strassburg, the author of a Latin chronicle of
that time, — "Anno Domini MCCCXVII in virgilia
sancti Andreæ, sepultus est Henricus dictus Frauenlob in Maguntia, in ambitu majoris Ecclesiæ, juxta
scalas honorifice valde: qui deportatis fuit a mulieribus
ab hospitio usque ad locum sepulturæ et lamentiones
    querelæ maximæ auditæ fuerunt ab eis, propter
laudes infinitas, quas imposuit omni generi fœmineo
in dictaminibus suis.   Tanta etiam ibi copia fuit
vina fusa in sepulchrum suum, quod circumfluebat per

totum ambitum ecclesiæ cantica canticorum dictavit Teutoniæ quæ vulgaritur dicuntur, Unser Frauen Lied, et multa alia bona."

The following few strophes from a Latin version of this great Lay must conclude our illustrations of the Lay-form, and may at the same time serve to show in what manner some of the learned Minnesinger — for the Latin is doubtless from Frauenlob himself — know how to use the wonderful rhyme-capacities of the Latin language.

FROM FRAUENLOB'S CANTICA CANTICORUM.

Ey, in superno trono
Heram vidi fregnantem,
Stupore cunctis tono
Aureolam gestantem.
Hyans ab onerari
Processit summa bona
Gimmas bis sex, ut fari,
Gestavit in corona.

Contra nature jura
Virgo pura
En, quem erat paritura,
Quem ymo que gestavit,
Præ se vidit sedere,
Lucere
In septem lucernis
Vidit tamen divisum
Hunc agni sub figura
Florigero Syon in monte.

. . . . . .

Hilaria
Vinaria
In cellaria
Te rex regnum introduxit,
Illuxit.
Salutans
Te dulciter inebrians divino

Popino
Tuo vino
Magne dulcedinis, dulci lacte
Neminem
Refutans.

.   .   .   .   .   .

Quam diurnum solarium,
Virgo, tibi sacrarium !
Tua forma formosa,
Plus tronis speciosa,
Quorum clangor est, " corone rosa ! "
Feliciter,
Qui circiter
Dextram primis quiescit.
Pomulum, quod gestas, jam maturescit,
Decor florum ultrolibet ridescit,
Quorum ora perlavit ros
Ad loquendum sermones hos :
Super omnes hec virgo dilectat nos.

CHAPTER III.

THE DIVINE MINNESONG.

THE Minnesinger century witnessed probably the intensest and sincerest devotion to the worship of the Virgin Mary in the whole history of the Catholic Church, a worship expressed in the vast number of paintings and poems in her glorification whereof we have record. That whole period, indeed, was one of fervent religious feeling stimulated by the Crusades, and naturally chose the Virgin for the chief object of worship, as the whole knightly spirit of that age was one of devotion to woman. The pure love — for Minne is *pure* love — of woman has never, in the history of literature, been so exclusively made the topic of poetry as it was during that century of the Minnesinger; it is the absorbing theme of the poets of that time, and its highest expression was attained in those poems that were addressed to the woman of all women, — Mary, the mother of Jesus.

Of the many Minnelieder addressed to the Virgin we have preserved to us examples of both kinds, lays and songs. Chief among them are the Lay by Walther von der Vogelweide, and the "Great Hymn" by Gottfried von Strassburg.

The latter is probably the finest of all the Minnelieder — worldly and sacred — of that period. Rank-

ing next to these two there is, however, another poem
to the Virgin, not to be classified strictly under the
general title of Minnelieder, but still the production
of a famous Minnesinger, and withal a poem of wondrous beauty, which for two centuries kept its hold
upon the people, and which deserves mention here.
This is Conrad von Wurzburg's "Golden Smithy," a
poem written in the narrative metre.

In this "Golden Smithy" the poet represents himself
as a goldsmith, working all manner of precious stones
and gold into a glorious ornament for the Queen of
Heaven, by gathering into his poem all possible images and similes from the world of nature, from sacred
and profane history and fable, and from all the virtues
and graces of mankind. It is a poem of wonderful
splendor, and has a great smoothness of diction. "If,"
says the poet in the opening of the poem, "in the
depth of the smithy of my heart I could melt a poem
out of gold, and could enamel the gold with the glowing ruby of pure devotion, I would forge a transparent, shining, and sparkling praise of thy worth, thou
glorious empress of heaven. Yet, though my speech
should fly upward like a noble eagle, the wings of my
words could not carry me beyond thy praise. Marble and adamant shall be sooner penetrated by a
straw, and the diamond by molten lead, than I attain
the height of the praise that belongs to thee. Not
until all the stars have been counted, and the dust of
the sun and the sand of the sea and the leaves of the
trees, can thy praise be properly sung."

But even this poem is far surpassed in beauty every-
way by the one generally known as Gottfried von

Strassburg's "Great Hymn." Indeed, Conrad himself modestly confesses this in his "Golden Smithy,"
when he regrets that he does not "sit upon the green
clover bedewed with sweet speech, on which sat
worthily Gottfried von Strassburg, who, as a most
artistic smith, worked a golden poem, and praised
and glorified the Holy Virgin in much better strain."

There is, indeed, a wondrous beauty in this hymn
ascribed to Gottfried von Strassburg, a beauty much
akin to that of his own Strassburg Cathedral, which
was begun about the same time.

"It is," says Van der Hagen, "the very glorification of love (Minne) and of Minnesong; it is the heavenly bridal song, the mysterious Solomon's Song,
which mirrors its miraculous object in a stream of
deep and lovely images, linking them all together into
an imperishable wreath; yet even here in its pro-
fundity and significance of an artistic and numerously
rhymed construction, always clear as crystal, smooth,
and graceful."

The noteworthy part of this poem is the symmetry
of its construction in the general conception and idea
of the poem and the wonderfully artistic manner in
which that symmetry is also made manifest and
heightened by the sensuous elements of rhythm,
rhyme, word-sound, and that peculiar refrain, which
has elsewhere been spoken of as occurring in "Tristan
and Isolde," and the nature whereof is so weirdly or
sweetly effective in music when — not a whole musical
phrase is strictly repeated, which is simply the regular
refrain, but — a short passage reoccurs unexpectedly,
though with thorough musical logic, or in another

key, or so slightly varied as to recall the previous phrase and yet seem not the same.

The hymn opens with the poet's exhortation to all those who desire to listen to his song of God's great love, to endeavor its attainment by unremitting exertion, and to pray for him, the poet, who has so little striven to gain it for himself. Then throwing his plaint aside, the poet calls upon the heavens and Christ to bend down and listen to his tuneful lays in praise of Christ's sweet mother; and now with increasing fervor begins that wonderful praise —

"Thou bloom of rose, thou lily grace!"

The tone is slightly lowered and calmed down as the poet passes to recount the bliss and grace of her worship, and rises again as he proceeds to call upon all things in earth and heaven to praise her; and finally upon herself to rejoice in her passing glory. The sound of the first chant of praise is once more heard, —

"Thou of pure grace a clear, fair vase!"

And the poet turns from her glorification of the mother to that of her son.

The praise takes the same form of language, —

"Thou cool, thou cold, thou warmth, thou heat!"

with occasional recurring of the same images, and rises in power until it and the whole poem, indeed, ascending to the praise of God himself, swell into highest intensity, —

"God of thee speaking, God of thee saying!"

The very words seem to shake with fervor of emotion, and by repetition of utterance to sob out their inability to utter his supreme love.

The gradual toning down of the poem from this intensity is sensuously executed with marvelous skill. At first one of the repetitions of the line, —

"God of thee speaking, God of thee saying," —

is left out in a stanza. In the next one another one is left out, and the first one changed, moreover: —

"God of thee speaking repentance raises; " —

the unusual feminine rhyme being yet, however, retained. But in the next one the masculine rhyme takes its place again, and in all the following stanzas the rhythm retains its even flow. A few verses lead to the notable close of the poem, which expires in a long drawn sigh.

It is, of course, impossible to render in a translation all this sensuous beauty and art of rhythm, rhyme, and word-sound. I can say only that I have done my best.

There are several manuscripts existing of this poem, but each one defective, though not materially so. The whole of the poem has undoubtedly been preserved, with the exception of a very few small passages that I have ventured to fill up in the translation. In arranging the order of the stanzas I have followed Van der Hagen's suggestion, which indeed the poem itself confirms as correct.

Who the real author of this wonderful hymn is, has remained unknown. It was ascribed to Gottfried von Strassburg, until in 1859 the late Ernest Pfeiffer conclusively demonstrated it to be not Gottfried's hymn to which Conrad von Wurzburg refers, but a hymn from an unknown Minnesinger *after the man-*

ner of Gottfried's. Professor Bartsch, the learned editor of Brockhaus' edition of the Minnesinger, informs
me that since then it is considered a settled matter
that Gottfried was not the author of it.

HYMN TO THE VIRGIN.

I.

— Ye who your life would glorify,
And float in bliss with God on high,
    There to dwell nigh
  His peace and love's salvation ;
— Who fain would learn how to enroll
All evil under your control,
    And rid your soul
  Of many a sore temptation :
— Give heed unto this song of love,
  And follow its sweet story ;
Then will its passing sweetness prove
Unto your hearts a wingèd dove,
    And upward move
  Your souls to bliss and glory.

II.

— Ye who would hear what you have ne'er
Heard spoken, now incline your ear
    And listen here
  To what my tongue unfoldeth ;
— Yea, list to the sweet praise and worth
Of her who to God's child gave birth ;
    Wherefore on earth
  God as in heaven her holdeth.

— E'en as the air when fresh bedewed
  Bears fruitful growth, so to man
She bears an ever fruitful mood :
Never so chaste bloom of heart's blood,
    So true and good,
  Was born by mortal woman.

III.

— Who of God's love would hunter be
Must have a hunter's heart, which he
    Can fearlessly
  On hunting-ground keep steady,
— He must have hero's strength and pace
If he pure love would win in race,
    Must watch each phase
  And be for battle ready.
— He must do both by night and day
  To win this God's-love's favor ;
It goeth not sleeping on the way,
It must be forced where'er its stay,
    Straight made the prey
  Of pure and strong endeavor.

IV.

— Yea, God's love is of soaring mood
And yet most humble, true, and good ;
    Who never would
  By deeds gain its possession,
— To him it never will appear ;
Nor will he by its love, I fear,
    Be wounded e'er,
  Or feel its blessed passion.

6

— It is so blessed in its mood,
  It fain would be revealing
In every heart the highest good,
And dearest bloom of heart's own blood:
    Who in its flood
  Bathes not, is void of feeling.

v.

— Who to God's love are strangers, they
With seeing eyes see not the day;
    Of them we say
  They're children of the earth still.
— But who God's love in truth possess
Are named God's children, and men bless
    Their names always,
  And worship their great worth still.
— Their fruitful fruit heaven's fruitful rain
  And blessed dews doth capture.
God's blessings so on them doth gain
That always follow in his train:
    They must attain
  His glory's greatest rapture.

vi.

— He whom God's love could ne'er compel,
Never in rare delight could dwell;
    Good thought's strong spell
  Ne'er broke for him life's prison.
— He whom God's love has never found
Is like a shadow on the ground,
    And does confound
  Life, wisdom, sense, and reason.

— He whom God's blessed love did raise
　　Soul, heart, and body never,
Of grace is but an empty vase ;
Sheer blind is his heart's mirror-glass ;
　　　His body was
　　Dead and stays dead forever.

VII.

— Aye, that 'tis I who sing of love,
Whom yet so little it doth move,
　　　Must surely prove
　　That I deserve men's pity ;
— Yea, had it ever tried my heart
As it those pure hearts tempts, that part
　　　Ne'er from the start
　　And pathway to God's city,
— I loudly might the praise declare
Of that God's love enchanting ;
Now must I of my speech despair,
Since in my days its image fair
　　　Rarely came where
　　My parchèd soul lay panting.

VIII.

— Could I be helped by passionate plaint
I should complain without restraint
　　　That I ne'er went
　　To hunt love's sacred passion ;
— Wherewith I should have won that high
Sweet love, that nevermore can die ;
　　　Me cheated the lie,
　　That cheateth all transgression.

—I dreamed and did not want to see,
For I am such a dreamer,
Who inward blind sees outwardly
As happens to all fools.   Ah me,
    Who never see
And whose joy is mere glimmer.

IX.

— O faithful God, commiserate
And pity my low-sunken state ;
    Lo, for thy great
Sweet grace I ever languish,
— For, Lord, my sins more countless be
Than the waters in the Bodensea ;
    This stirs in me
Repentance and great anguish,
— For I have in my life's short day
For thy love made no proffer.
Ah well, I may confess and say
Towards thy love I was alway
    A coward, aye
And justly now I suffer.

X.

—Wherever virtuous hearts yet blaze,
Who hear of these my plaintive lays :
    O, may they raise
Their voice to God in heaven
— And to his mother, the divine,
That to this parchèd heart of mine
    The living wine
Of true remorse be given.

— I ask this for the sainted blood
  That He shed for each sinner ;
Thus may I of that love of God
Which stirs anew each heart's dried flood
      In joyful mood,
  Be yet successful winner.

XI.

— And now my plaint I'll throw aside,
Whilst praise on praise I build and wide
      Expand the tide
  Of love all pure and holy ;
— Of never-ending purity,
From sin and all those passions free,
      That shamefully
  Seek to possess us solely.
— Aye, let us silence sin and dare —
  God's gracious love loud chanting, —
To rid us of its loathsome care,
And unto God upraise our prayer ;
      His love so rare
  Into our hearts transplanting.

XII.

— Ye fruitful heavens, from your ways
Bend down to hear the tuneful lays
      I sing in praise
  Of her, the sainted maiden,
— Who unto us herself has shown
Of modest life a crown and throne ;
      Whose love has flown
  O'er many a heart grief-laden.

— Thou, too, O Christ, thine ear incline,
　　To this my adoration,
　In honor of that mother thine,
Who ever blessed must stay and shine :
　　For she 's the shrine
　　Of God's whole vast creation.

XIII.

— Her praise will rise fruitful, I ween,
As leaves, grass, flowers, and clover seen
　　O'er meadow's green,
　When fruitful rains them brighten.
— It must refresh our parched heart's gloom,
E'en as the dews of heaven, perfume
　　Each fruitful bloom ;
　It must our souls enlighten,
— E'en as lights up the morn with red
　When the new sun has risen.
It must bear us the living bread,
That e'en gives life to souls all dead
　　With need and dread ;
　And free us from sin's prison.

XIV.

— Cleanse us, thou clean and fruitful mood,
Of laughing roses the playful blood,
　　Thou climbing flood,
　Thou flowing honey's flavor,
— Cleanse us that we thy praise may move,
And tie us with the ties of love,
　　That we above
　May be looked on with favor.

— Pour out thy fruitfullest love — drink,
  To quench our heart's wild fever;
So that our souls may never sink,
And ever from life's sweetness shrink;
       O, make us think
   Of true repentance ever.

xv.

— Light up our hearts, thou daylight calm,
In the fire of love the scent of balm,
       Thou blooming palm,
   That in our love's heat groweth.
— Delight us, thou delightful guest;
Lay sin forever in us waste,
       Each thought unchaste
   Check, love, that in us floweth.
— That gracious blessing with us share
   Which erst an angel brought thee,
With blessed speech as he drew near;
That same sweet greeting bring us here
       God's messenger
   Bore with him as he sought thee.

xvi.

— Thou bloom of rose, thou lily grace,
Thou glorious Queen in that high place
       Where ne'er the face
   Of woman shone before thee;
— Thou sweet heart's love 'gainst all distress,
Thou gladness in sore bitterness,
       Thou, whom all bless,
   Our souls for aye adore thee.

— Thy womb, the living God's recess,
　　Now blessèd is in story,
E'en as the sunlight through the glass,
Better and sweeter and no less
　　　　With love did pass
　　Through thee the Christ of glory.

XVII.

— Thou rosy vale, thou violet plain,
Thou pleasure bearing heart's great gain,
　　　　Thou Hero-Queen,
　　Thou sweet God's joy to low man.
— Thou light-diffusing morning-red.
Thou steadfast friend in need and dread ;
　　　　The living bread
　　Thou bor'st, O queenly woman,
— That many a gloomy heart and cold
　　Lit up and set a-glowing
With sweetest love most manifold ;
Such wondrous strength is in its hold :
　　　　Its praise is told
　　The universe o'erflowing.

XVIII.

— Thou lovely, golden flower-glow,
Thou bloom'st on every maiden's brow ;
　　　　And glory's glow
　　E'en like a robe floats on thee.
— Thou art the blooming heaven-branch,
Which blooming blooms in many a grange,
　　　　Great care and strange
　　God lavished, Maid, upon thee.

— Hence highest praise to thee is brought,
   And in thy glory chanted.
Of many hearts the gladsome thought
Rings many a song with sweetness fraught :
    Thus hast thou caught
   And thus thou hast them daunted.

XIX.

— Thou sheen of flowers through clover place,
Thou *lignum aloe's* blooming phase,
    Thou sea of grace
  Where man seeks blessed landing.
— Thou roof to rapture high and blest,
Through which no rain has ever passed,
    Thou goodly rest,
  Whose end is without ending.
— Thou to help-bearing strength a tower
  Against all hostile evils.
Thou parriest many a stormy shower,
Which o'er us cast in darkest hour,
    The hell worm's power
  And other ruthless devils.

XX.

— Thou art a sun, a moon, a star ;
'Tis thou canst give all good and mar,
    Yea, and debar
  Our enemies' great cunning.
— That power God to thee hath given,
That living life, that light of heaven:
    Hence see we even
  Thy praise from all lips running.

— Thou'st won the purest, noblest fame
  In all the earth's long story,
That e'er attached to worldly name ;
It floweth brightly without grame ;
      All hearts the same
  Adore its lasting glory.

XXI.

— Thou of all sweetness sweetest shine,
Thou sweeter than e'er earth grew wine,
      The sweetness thine
  Must bloom for me forever.
— Thou art the sweet love-drink of the skies
Whereof e'en God quaffed sweetest joys.
      Yea, siren's voice
  Such sweetness warbled never.
— Thou goest through ear, thou goest through eye,
  Our heart and soul awaking.
There rousest thou transporting joy ;
All sadness leaves when thou art by,
      Thou art the high
  Reward of love unshaking.

XXII.

— O beauty o'er all beauty's birth !
Never rare stone, or herb, or earth,
      Or man bring forth
  Such wondrous beauty, maiden !
— So great thy beauty's lustrous light :
Upon our hearts it pours a bright
      Stream of delight,
  And radiance as of Aiden.

— It blooms in every place and phase
  Still sweet and ever sweeter.
I scarce dare look upon thy face,
So wonderful its glorious grace ;
    'Tis God's own face :
  I greet Him when I greet her.

XXIII.

O o'er all virtues virtue fair !
O endless youth in youth's spring-year !
    Well may youth bear
  Thy praise and sing thy favor.
— The heavens and the heaven-begot,
All saints that near the great God float
    Are blind, I wot,
  In heart and true endeavor,
— If to that sweetest worthiness
  They bring not homage lowly,
Which God unto thee given has
With many another gift and grace ;
    Whence all men bless
  Thee, maid, so pure and holy.

XXIV.

— Thou gem, thou gold, thou diamond glow,
Thou cream-white milk, red ivory, O !
    Thou honey-flow,
  In heart and mouth dissolving ;
— Of fruitful virtue a noble grove,
The lovely bride of God above —
    Thou sweet, sweet love,
  Thou hour with bliss revolving.

Of chastity thou whitest snow,
   A grape of chaste and sure love,
A clover-field of true love's glow,
Of grace a bottomless ocean's flow ;
      Yea, more, I trow :
   A turtle-dove of pure love.

XXV.

God thee hath clothed with raiments seven ;
On thy pure body drawn from heaven
      Hath put them even
   When thou wast first created.
The first one *chastity* is named,
The second is as *virtue* famed,
      The third is claimed
   As *courtesy*, well mated.
The fourth dress is *humility*,
   The fifth is known as *pity ;*
The sixth one, *faith*, clings close to thee,
The seventh, noble *modesty*,
      Leads gratefully
Thee in the path of duty.

XXVI.

— With fair chaste hands thou art arrayed,
Who wast not either wife or maid ;
     Thus is it said
   Of thee, O noble woman.
— Chaste was thy seeing, chaste thy sight,
Thy hearing chaste and all times right,
      Thy speech flowed bright
And chaste as that of no man.

— Chaste was thy drink, chaste was thy food,
  Chaste were thy sense and feeling.
Chaste was thy heart, chaste was thy mood,
Chaste every movement of thy blood,
    Wherein the flood
  Of God's love poured man-healing.

XXVII.

— Thou sun, thou moon, thou star so fair,
God took thee from his own side there
    Here to prepare
  The birth of Christ within thee.
— For that his lovèd child and thine,
Which is our life and life's sunshine,
    Our bread and wine,
  To stay chaste He did win thee ;
— So that sins' thorns could never touch
  Thy fruitful virtue's branches.
His burning love for thee did vouch,
He kept thee from all sins that crouch :
    A golden couch
  Secured by his love's trenches.

XXVIII.

— Thou body pure of high degree,
Ne'er woman's form the earth did see
    Fashioned like thee
  So graceful sweet and tender.
— Maria, honor's fruitful tree,
Most holy *templum domini*,
    That stands through thee
  Firm and beyond surrender,

— Thou origin of all the sweet
  Delights of earth and heaven,
The Godhead made thy heart its seat,
To all of us a benefit;
      Hence where we meet
  Our thanks to thee are given.

XXIX.

I speak of thee in my best strain:
No mother e'er such child may gain,
      No child attain
  So pure a mother ever.
He chose what his own nature was;
His glorious Godhead chose as case
      The purest vase
  Of flesh and bone's endeavor,
That woman ever on her heart
  'Tween earth and heaven did treasure.
In thee lay hidden every part
That ever did from virtue start;
      Of bliss thou art
  An unexhausted measure.

XXX.

— Thou growing love for every woe,
Thou of God's grace the dearest flow,
      Sure none may know,
  But one, thy passing splendor;
— And that of our dear Christ, thy son,
Who by his love our love has won,
      Whom as God's own
  All mankind homage render.

— Who woman's sweetness ne'er has known,
   Who is orphan and widow;
And though all countries He has won,
Yet so much grace on thee is thrown :
     Thou art alone
   A tower on danger's meadow.

XXXI.

— Thou art a light, an origin
Of life, change ne'er can enter in,
     'Twast thou drov'st sin
   From us and wicked terror.
— 'Twast thou who with thy warm sunshine
And with that fruitful light of thine,
     Thou heavenly shrine,
   Quick didst dispel all error.
— Thou open'dst us the door of grace,
   That, alas! from beginning
Was closed on us, poor souls always ;
Thou hold'st us to find the right place :
     Hence all our days
   We raise thy praise prayer-bringing.

XXXII.

— To worship, Lady, thee, is bliss ;
And fruitful hours ne'er pass amiss
     To heart that is
   So sweet a guest's host-mansion.
— He who thee but invited hath
Into his heart's loved love with faith,
     Must live and bathe
   In endless bliss-expansion.

— To worship thee stirs up in man
A love now tame, now a passion.
To worship thee doth waken then
Love e'en in those love ne'er could gain :
        Thus now amain
    Shines forth thy love's concession.

XXXIII.

— To worship, Lady, thee, doth hate
'Gainst lazy hosts in us create
        And makes us sate
    With sin and every evil.
— To worship, Lady, thee, is bliss
That ne'er is checked by wickedness,
        Or sin's stol'n kiss,
    Or cunning of the devil.
— To worship, Lady, thee, doth wake
    The hardest soul from slumber.
To worship thee must surely shake
Or man's or woman's hearts and break
        Them to forsake
    The sins that them encumber.

XXXIV.

— To worship, Lady, thee, doth teach
Pray'r to drenched courage and numbed speech,
        Yea, and fires each
    Cold heart with heavenly rapture.
— To worship thee, O Lady, can
Teach many an erring sinful man
        How from sin's ban
    He still his soul may capture.

— To worship thee is e'en a branch
On which the soul's life bloometh.
To worship thee makes bold and stanch
The weakest soul on sin's hard bench ;
God it doth wrench
From hell and in heaven roometh.

XXXV.

— To worship, Lady, thee, so good,
Who does it truly, in his mood
God pours love's blood :
Thou art so pure and holy.
— Who worships thee doth honor Him
And his great love's outpouring stream :
It is one scheme,
One love, one essence solely,
— One steady will and but one power,
One no, one yea, one summon.
No tempest can its bloom deflower,
Eternity doth o'er it lower ;
Hence praises shower
On thee, O sainted woman.

XXXVI.

— Then praise both men and women thy name,
And what of mother's womb e'er came,
Both wild and tame,
With warm heartfelt devotion.
— Then praise thee now what living lives,
Whatever heaven's dew receives,
Runs, flows, or cleaves
Through forest or through ocean.

7

—— Then praise thee now the fair star-shine,
  The sun and the moon gold-glowing ;
Then praise thee the four elements thine ;
Yea, be thou blessed by me and mine,
    Thou cheering wine,
  Thou stream with grace o'erflowing.

XXXVII.

—— Then praise thee God who created thee,
And who listens so lovingly
    To all men's plea,
  Their joy and eke their sadness ;
—— Then praise thee loud the angels' choir,
All virgins of thy vast empire,
    And higher and higher
  The martyrs' passing gladness ;
—— Then praise thee now thou God-love's stream,
  God's heaven's glorious beauty,
And all the beings that supreme
Move there ; yea, e'en the cherubim
    And seraphim :
  Praise thee in blissful duty.

XXXVIII.

—— Now praise thee, sweetest purity,
  All that e'er death through God did see ;
    To-day to thee
  Be praise by all tongues chanted ;
—— Now praise thee blooming roses aye
And modest maiden's chaste display ;
    Thy praise to-day
  O'er all the world be planted.

— Now honor thee, O blessed hoard,
Thee, joy-inspiring fountain,
Who here on earth live in the Lord;
To-day of thy sweet praise each word
Ring in accord
From every vale and mountain.

XXXIX.

— O mother pure, learn now how nigh
To God thy ever blessed boy
A throne on high
For thee did choose and borrow.
— Thou shalt in radiant pleasures flow,
Thou shalt to richest glory go,
There learn to know
A life that has no sorrow.
— That pure, chaste image of thy grace
Shall in the bloom of pleasure
Rejoice for aye in every place;
The living sunshine did embrace
Thee, honor's vase,
His chosen greatest treasure.

XL.

— Rejoice, then, Lady of the skies;
Rejoice, thou God-love's paradise;
Rejoice, thou prize
Of sweetest roses growing.
— Rejoice, thou birth of sacred plan;
Rejoice, that every race and clan,
Women and man
Pray to thy love o'erflowing.

— Rejoice that thou with God dost show
  So many things in common :
His yea thy yea, his no thy no ;
Endless ye mingle in one flow ;
      Small and great, lo !
He shares with thee, sweet woman.

XLI.

— Rejoice now, Lady, that thou'rt known
As highest saints on heaven's throne ;
      And that thou'st won
  All the angels' sweetness for thee.
— Rejoice now, that in highest grade
Of heaven's joys thou'st been arrayed ;
      Rejoice, O maid,
  That all hearts now adore thee ;
— And that sweet thanks arise to thee
  And all thoughts on thee centre.
Rejoice now thousand hours with me
That thou no more canst wounded be,
      Or unhealthy
  Earth's pains thy soul can enter.

XLII.

— Rejoice now, Lady, that God's suit
Chose thee, his anger to compute,
      Through that sweet fruit,
  Which thy womb bore unto man.
— Rejoice now, that that Christ of bliss,
Thy child, thy God, thy Father is,
      And that thou'rt this
  Bright mirror to all women.

— Rejoice now that thy loving blood
  From heavy sorrow's pressure
Has liberated many a mood;
Drowning all grief with flowing flood:
        Rejoice thou good
  And blessedest eye-pleasure.

XLIII.

— Rejoice now that unmild regret
Has dampened ne'er that mildness yet,
        That thou hast set
  For the repentant ready.
— Thou to the naked clothes hast brought
And given them many a wholesome thought;
        'Tis writ, I wot:
  Who follows thee, sweet Lady,
— To him shall not be help denied,
  God's own assent full-given.
Hence rolls thy praise so far and wide
That no one can transcend its tide,
        Or from it hide,
  Whether on earth or heaven.

XLIV.

— Rejoice now, Lady, that thy sweet
Blessed body never gave retreat
        To sin's swift feet
  In heart or senses ever,
— Hence may'st thou well thy thanks upraise,
For it is worthy of all praise:
        Yea, God's great grace
  Was ever thy love's lever.

— Into thy heart He poured his love,
    And into thy pure bosom,
Wherein no one can equal prove
To thee, but thy sweet son, whose love
        Is one vast grove
    Of honor-bearing blossom.

XLV.

— Rejoice now, thou sweet sugar-plant,
That God his angel Gabriel sent,
        With high intent:
    A chosen emissary,
— His greeting forth to thee to bear,
That rose so sweetly on thine ear:
        As he drew near
    His feet flew light and airy,
Thus thou God's greeting did'st receive;
    His art thou now, sweet maiden,
Thy womb shall now in bliss conceive,
Cast then away all thoughts that grieve;
        Thou shalt achieve
    Freedom to the sin-laden.

XLVI.

— Rejoice now, sweet advice in need,
That of his living bliss the seed
        God sowed indeed
    Into thy heart's sweet furrow.
— Rejoice now, holy paradise,
That He, in turtle-dove's winged guise,
        Thy friend and prize
    Brought to us in our sorrow.

— Through that all saintly ear of thine
  To under thy fair bosom.
Whereof thou blessed must stay and shine
The queen of all the hosts divine ;
    The holy shrine
  Of every pleasure's blossom.

XLVII.

— Rejoice now, that that heart of thine
The Holy Ghost's great love made pine
    And haste to join,
  Thy own sweet love caressing.
— Rejoice now, thou salvation's throne,
That thou gav'st birth to Him, who won
    Our cause, thy son,
  Our Saviour and our blessing.
— Rejoice now, thou sweet purity,
  That thou so pure, amylèd,
Conceivd'st the Christ who made us free ;
Whence all men's tongues recount of thee
    Praise passingly
  That God so on thee smilèd.

XLVIII.

— Rejoice now, O thou sunshine mild,
That on thy blessed breasts there smiled
    God's little child :
  Its earthly destination.
— Rejoice that then drew near to thee
From foreign lands the wise kings three,
    Noble and free,
  To bring their adoration

— To thee and to that blessed child,
  With many a graceful off'ring.
Rejoice now, that the star beguiled
And to that place their pathway smiled,
    Where with thy child
  They worshipped thy sweet suff'ring.

XLIX.

— Rejoice now, thou pure mother's bairn,
That thou to heaven shalt discern
        Jesus' return,
    To whom thou birth hast given.
— Rejoice now, that his grace He poured
Often upon thee ere He soared,
        And thee restored
    To the sweet peace of heaven.
— Rejoice, that thou wert free the fate
    To witness men prepared Him.
How full of love and without hate
He on the wind's light feathers sat,
        Godlike in that,
    When loud the crowd declared Him.

L.

— Rejoice now, fruitful life benign,
That thou art called to help assign
        Judgment divine
    To pitiful human sinners
— Upon that dreadful judgment day,
When God accusant shall display
        To grim array
    Of poor and rich demeanors

—His blessèd wounds, whose mouths still speak,
  With fresh red blood, o'erflowing.
For He was wounded for our sake;
This causes many a one to quake:
      Alas, the weak,
    Alas, the dole there growing.

LI.

— O Maria, purest worthiness,
What has been chanted in thy praise
      Is sweet always
    Beyond all other singing.
—' Thou fill'st our body and soul with joy,
Thou lift'st up heart and senses high,
      Now far, now nigh,
    And ever pleasure bringing.
— Thou bloomest fair in flower-wise,
  In heart and soul bright-shining,
Thou art so true a paradise,
Of rapture a rose that never dies,
      Of bliss a prize,
    Of grace a rod divining.

LII.

— Thou of pure grace a clear, fair vase!
Of steady virtue an adamas,
      A mirror glass
    Of bliss to bliss surrendered.
——Thou fortune's and salvation's host,
Thou love-seed of the Holy Ghost;
      To all sin lost
    Thy image was engendered.

— On sacred place, where at God's call
God's Son sank down from heaven.
Like on the flowers sweet rain doth fall,
Such gentle sweetness He to all,
    Whom reached his call,
Early and late hath given.

LIII.

— Now have I praised the mother Thine,
O sweet, fair Christ, that form divine
    And honor's shrine
In which Thou wast created.
— And loud I'll now praise Thee, O Lord;
Yea did I not 'twould check my word:
    Thy praise has soared
And with all things been mated.
— Seven hours each day Thy praise shall now
By me in prayer be chanted.
This well belongs to Thee, I trow,
For Thou art every virtue's prow;
    From all grief Thou
To us relief hast granted.

LIV.

— With Thy name now my praise accord,
For Thou alone didst make me, Lord;
    Thy praise has soared
And still soars up to heaven.
— Thus, Lord, I praise Thee, that Thou art
A true Lord and true Christ, whose heart
    Contains no part
Of sin's polluting leaven.

— It is in all the virtues clear,
   Transparent as pure crystal.
It changes not the breadth of a hair,
It is straightforward, true, and fair,
      And *debonnaire*
   As that of purest vestal.

LV.

— I praise Thee, Father, Christ, and Lord,
That e'en the sinner Thou hast heard:
      His simple word
   Of pledged repentance trusting.
— Hence be Thou praised, Lord, night and day,
By all the praise I sinner may
      Raise in my lay,
   Or tongue to speak be lusting.
— For Thou each human heart dost see,
   Nothing to Thee is latent.
Thou knowest the sea's depth's mystery,
Yea, all men's mouths may speak to Thee,
      Is and shall be
   Now and forever patent.

LVI.

— Thus praise I now, O Lord, Thy death,
Which in our dreadful agony hath
      Brought helpful breath
   To every wretched sinner;
— Redeeming us from shame and sin
And misery, that is their kin:
      Thus hast Thou been
   Ever our comfort-gleaner.

— Hence what hath breath shall now unfurl
Thy glory, never-resting :
Woman and man, yea, boy and girl,
All that doth fly, flow, run, or whirl,
    Crawl, glide, or curl,
  As now so everlasting.

LVII.

— God, Thou the origin of all good,
Or deep or high, or long or broad ;
    It knoweth the road,
  Sweet thoughts into hearts bringing ;
— It floweth from the land of love ;
Hail Him, into whose heart it drove:
    His heart's a grove
  Of laughing and sweet singing ;
— Whate'er the world to him may show
  From woe turns into pleasure.
So sweetly maketh his heart glow,
Thy sweetness-bearing and gushing flow :
    For to men, lo !
  Thy goodness has no measure.

LVIII.

— Thou art that gentle gentleness
Which every gentle heart doth bless ;
    No heart's sadness
  Found rapture yet more tender
— Than that most gentle sweetness thine ;
Its passing bliss for all that pine
    Is a divine
  True doctrine of vast splendor.

— Yet did that sweetness never flow,
   But o'er pure hearts that flutter;
Them stirs it to voluptuous glow
And draweth grace anew to grow;
       Its conquering flow
   Stills all the sighs they utter.

LIX.

— Thou cool, thou cold, thou warmth, thou heat,
Thou rapture's circle's central seat,
       Who does not meet
   With Thee stays dead in sadness;
— Each day to him appears a year,
Seldom his thoughts wear green bloom's gear;
       He doth appear
   Forever without gladness.
— Thou art most truly our heart's shine,
   Our sun wide joy-inspiring;
A sweet heart's love for all that pine,
For all the sad a joyful shrine,
       A spring divine
   For the thirsty and desiring.

LX.

— Thou love and dear, Thou love and sweet!
Never a love such love may meet;
       Thy love men greet
   As love that ever bloometh.
— Thou art beloved by maid and wife;
Thee loveth every virtuous life;
       Thy love all strife
   Within our heart o'ercometh.

— Thou art beloved by earth and sea,
By fire, air, storm, and weather,
By heaven's appalling majesty,
And by the blushing flowers so wee :
Aye, love for Thee
Breathes the remotest ether.

LXI.

— Thou of so many pure hearts the hold,
So many a pure maid's sweetheart bold,
All Thee enfold
With love bright, pure, and yearning.
Thou art caressed by many a mood,
Caressed by many a heart's warm blood ;
Thou art so good,
So truthful and love-burning ;
— Caressed by all the stars that soar,
By sun and moon, Thou blessing !
Caressed by all the elements four ;
O ne'er caressed so was afore,
Nor shall be more,
Sweetheart, by love's caressing.

LXII.

— Thou full moon, Thou full star so fair,
Thy light what heart an hour would spare,
That loves to wear
Thy virtue's fullest measure?
— Sure love for Thee must ever grow,
For Thou canst wondrous bliss bestow ;
Thou star, whose glow
Both heart and senses treasure.

— Thou lightest up, that no sunshine
  Nor star-shine can be brighter.
So mild, Lord, is Thy sweet love's wine,
Into whose hearts its glow doth shine,
    His heart's whole shrine
  With Thy love's joy grows lighter.

LXIII.

— Thou of so many a heart loveband,
Thou burning love o'er every land,
    World without end
  Was not made known love dearer.
— Thy love in living love doth grow;
Happy who strives to get its glow:
    His heart must flow
  To its rare rapture nearer.
— Thou bloometh in the soul's pure mood
  As in the sunlit pasture
A fruitful tree, graceful and good,
Whose flow'ry bloom laughs in the wood,
    Where every bud
  Opes to the dew its vesture.

LXIV.

— Deep is the wild sea's bottom's sweep,
But hundred thousand times more deep
    Is the vast sweep
  Of thy great pity; growing
— It reaches from the stars' high throne
Unto the bottomless ocean's moan;
    A comb o'erflown
  With the sweetest honey flowing.

— It floweth, flieth, and is blown
    Through many a wild adventure.
Thou art a God e'en to the bone,
Thy sweetness never change has known;
        Of seeds alone
    Thou art without a tainture.

LXV.

—Hence I, O sweetest God, praise Thee
For Thy commandments' purity,
        That changelessly
    Hold us to their attendance.
— Hence praise I Thee, that Thou art e'er
Where Thou art wanted, far or near,
        And that Thou dear
    Holdeth each heart's repentance.
— Hence praise I, sweet Lord Christ, that Thou
Ne'er from the poor did'st sever.
Thy sainted ear was e'er, I trow,
To their voice opened, and is now,
        And shall be so,
    World without end forever.

LXVI.

— Behold, O fruitful lovebloom, now
With virtue so imbued art Thou,
        So good, I trow,
    That what is due unto Thee
—N o speech of man can ever scan:
Not angel there, nor on earth man
        Or woman can   .
    Chant fitly what I owe Thee.

— Yet is it meet to raise a lay
  To Thy great love's endeavor ;
Which blooming casts an endless day
O'er all the world, and mankind ; aye,
    A joyful play
  To the good-hearted ever.

LXVII.

— Thou art that passing mercy, Lord,
Which high into the heavens has soared,
    And has explored
  Th' expanse of the wild ocean.
— Its deep abyss no bottom has,
Its length no man's mind can compass,
    What hours, alas !
  It ponders o'er the notion.
— Its grace was never yet so small
  As with the world to equal.
Its faithfulness no numbers call,
Its love fills mountains, vales, and all
    The lands that fall
  In undulating sequel.

LXVIII.

— Thou'rt called the living, saving grace ;
Through us Thou suffered'st death's embrace ;
    Yet didst Thou face
  Grim death with glad endeavor.
— Thou gladden'st us with Thy great dread,
To let us live Thou laid'st down dead ;
    Such faith was paid
  By no man to man ever.

8

—Since Adam from the earth was won,
　And by Thy hand created,
Never such noble faith was known,
Nor ever will its like be known ;
　　　Hence to Thy throne
　Praises rise unabated.

LXIX.

—Yea, Thou art sung night, noon, and morn,
The Lamb that all our sin has borne,
　　　Our misery worn,
　And death for us has suffered.
—We were too dear to Thee, I ween,
Thy gold Thou put'st upon mere skin :
　　　By all our kin
　Be praise then to Thee offered ;
—Unto Thy love, so pure alway,
　So sweet and so unchanging.
Hence must Thou ever blessèd stay,
Thou of pure hearts a sunlight-day,
　　　Thou wine so gay,
　Thou joy o'er all hearts ranging.

LXX.

—Yea, Thou art named the God of grace,
Without whose special power no phase
　　　Of life in space
　Had ever gained existence.
—What runneth, climbeth, sneaketh, or striveth,
What crawleth, twineth, flieth, or diveth,
　　　Yea, all that thriveth
　In earth and heaven's subsistence :

—Of all, the life to Thee is known,
　Thou art their food and banner ;
The lives of all are held alone
By Thee, O Lord ! upon Thy throne ;
　　Thus is well known
　Thy grace in every manner.

LXXI.

— Thou living light, Thou living aid,
Thou of all bliss the best man had :
　　Who could be glad
　Between the earth and heaven,
— Were't not for Thy love-bearing mood,
That cheereth every pure heart's blood,
　　And a full flood
　Of love to man has given?
— Thou gladdenest every angel's mood
　And every human being.
All that has flesh, or bone, or blood,
Is gladdened by Thy mercy's flood ;
　　Thou art so good,
　Thou love, and so farseeing !

LXXII.

— Thou at all times Thy arms didst hold
Open to draw us to Thy fold,
　　However cold
　Thy love we had offended.
— And all times when we do appear
Ready sin's fetters to forswear,
　　Thou draweth near ;
　And lo, our guilt is ended.

— Thou art so good, so very good,
　Nowhere such goodness gloweth;
Thy goodness living wonders would
Perform : it stirs the deadened mood,
　　That fruitful blood
From its hearts' chambers floweth.

LXXIII.

— Thee loves each bearing love-bloom's cell,
Thee loves each sense and heart's wild swell,
　　Thee loves full well
Each tender feeling bosom.
— Thee loves the body, sense, and life,
The soul we see fight in't life's strife,
　　For Thou art rife
With love's sweet-scented blossom.
— Those that love love Thou still art nigh,
　Their love-hearts Thou dost capture ;
Thy love extends from low to high,
Thou keep'st those that love love in joy ;
　　However coy,
Thou fill'st their hearts with rapture.

LXXIV.

— Thou art of love an origin,
But ne'er an end to love hast been ;
　　Thou art, I ween,
A chant that 's ever ringing.
— Men love Thee with a worthy joy ;
And wide and broad, and deep and high,
　　Without alloy
Floweth Thy love joy-bringing.

— Men love Thee, Lord, in wine and bread,
In gold and jewels precious.
Men love Thee in the scarlet-red,
Men love Thee unto death and dread ;
　　Wherever led,
Thou art so passing gracious.

LXXV.

— Thou art of burning love the glow,
Who loving poureth many a flow
　　Of sweetness, lo !
O'er hearts that in love languish ;
And sweetenest both their mind and mood
E'en as the dew the flow'ry wood ;
　　Thy love-bloom's blood
Driveth away all anguish.
— Those hearts that Thy hand tries, O Lord,
Must like true guests Thee love all,
Who art of living love a hoard,
Both here and in the sky adored ;
　　Hence, Thy sweet word
Blooms gloriously above all.

LXXVI.

— God, of Thee speaking ; God, of Thee saying,
Sweet love into our hearts keeps playing,
　　Whilst sore dismaying
The hating and the sinning.
— God, of Thee speaking ; God, of Thee saying,
Sweet beauty into our hearts keeps playing,
　　And teaches swaying
Thee with words sweet and winning.

God, of Thee speaking ; God of Thee saying,
   Maketh our hearts joy's palace ;
God, of Thee speaking ; God, of Thee saying,
The car of bliss moves on conveying
     Our souls' soft praying,
  To the realms of endless solace.

LXXVII.

God, of Thee speaking ; God, of Thee saying,
Freeth our hearts from thoughts sore-weighing,
     Whilst into't playing
  The Holy Spirit's beauty.
God, of Thee speaking ; God, of Thee saying,
Teaches the army of martyrs praying :
     Thou with them staying,
  Their tortures seem sweet duty.
God, of Thee speaking ; God, of Thee saying,
  Is half the kingdom of heaven.
God, of Thee speaking ; God, of Thee saying,
The kingdom of heaven unfolds displaying,
     Its splendors staying,
  Untinged by earthly leaven.

LXXVIII.

God, of Thee speaking ; God, of Thee saying,
Teacheth the heart its passions flaying,
     And stay waylaying
  The ever-watchful devil.
God, of Thee speaking ; God, of Thee saying,
Much strength and comfort keeps displaying ;
     And hearts thus staying,
  Are saved from every evil.

God, of Thee speaking ; God, of Thee saying,
   Is pleasure beyond all pleasure.
It moves our hearts, Thy grace surveying,
To keep with love Thy love repaying ;
      So sweetly swaying,
   Reveal'st Thou Thy love's treasure.

LXXIX.

God, of Thee speaking repentance raises
When they, who chant Thy wondrous praises,
      Use lying phrases:
   So purely Thy word gloweth.
It suffers less a lying mood
Than suffers waves the ocean's flood ;
      So pure and good
   Its changeless current floweth.
God, of Thee speaking doth attest
   Pure heart and chaste endeavor ;
It driveth the devil from our breast ;
O, well I know its soothing rest ;
      It is the zest
   Of Thy vast mercy's flavor.

LXXX.

— God, of Thee speaking brings grace aye,
And is the loveliest play to play,
      Which well I may
   Hold 'mongst all plays a treasure.
— Unto the body it giveth joy,
It doth the soul with great bliss cloy,
      Yea, fill and buoy
   Body and life with pleasure.

—Where'er are gathered two or three
  In Thy sweet love together,
Thou, Lord, art with them, where they be,
With Thy sweet grace and majesty,
      To keep them free
  From the influence of the nether.

LXXXI.

— Thou art of all pure hearts the play,
Thou com'st to them, whenever they
      Desire Thy stay :
  Thou bring'st love to so many.
— We have Thee there, we have Thee here,
We have Thee far, we have Thee near :
      A love more dear
  And sweeter, O, than any.
*— The very dearest love Thou art
  On which eye e'er did centre.
Into the heart Thou fling'st Thy dart ;
There greetest Thou Thy chaste sweetheart :
      On every mart
  Hearts beckon Thee to enter.

LXXXII.

— Of noble man the virtuous mood
Loveth to be both chaste and good ;
      And his heart's blood
  To grow in purity loveth,
— Through Thee, through purest of heart's blood ;
Thou art so pure, Thou art so good,
      Whom sin ne'er woo'd,
  And falseness never moveth.

— With genuine purity conceived
　　Thee the amylèd maiden.
Such birth, O Lord, was ne'er achieved,
So pure a birth no man received
　　That on earth lived,
　　Nor any saint of Aiden.

LXXXIII.

— Ah flower-crownèd flower bush !
Ah chaste heart untinged by a blush !
　　Ah sweet bride's flush !
　　Ah love with love o'ershowered !
— Ah heartily beloved hearts blood !
Ah goodness o'er all goodness good !
　　Ah noble mood,
　　Inward and outward flowered !
— Ah sweet view, ah sweet to look on !
Ah sweet to think of Thee, love !
Ah sweet to speak of Thee, sweet one !
Ah sweet to gaze such love upon !
　　Thy view alone
　　Drowneth all grief in me, love.

LXXXIV.

— Ah, of pure hearts Thou sweet *ami !*
Ah, how high praise becometh Thee,
　　Seeing that we
　　Through virtue rise e'er near Thee !
— Ah Emperor's child, ah kingly heir !
Ah Eagle of all eagles rare !
　　Thy tender care
　　Teaches us not to fear Thee.

— Keeping from grief all those who sought
Thy heart, with love abounding.
Ah, in the ear Thou sweet song brought!
Ah, in the heart Thou gladsome thought!
    Ah silver-wrought
Sweet harp forever sounding!

LXXXV.

— Ah child of God, ah sweet Christ Lord!
Ah o'er the world Thy sovereign word!
    Ah Thou who'st soared
A sun the morning meeting!
— Ah sweetest life, ah sweetest time!
Ah me, what happiness in each clime
    Doth climb and chime
Around Thee with fond greeting!
— Ah bonniest embrace and clasp!
Ah full of friendly rapture!
Ah ne'er did sweetness closer grasp
The heart of man into its clasp,
    With eager gasp,
And made a bonnier capture!

LXXXVI.

— Ah heart's sweetheart, ah full of grace!
Ah dear and ever dearer face!
    Ah sorrowless!
Ah medicine e'er aiding!
—Ah heart's wild breaking, ah heart's great dread!
Ah send us faith, till we are dead!
    Ah rose so red!
Bright rose that knows no fading!

—Ah youthfullest youth, ah youth-loving mood !
  Ah heart's-love so lightly soaring !
Ah growthfullest virtue, ah growth-loving good !
Ah Thou the genuine vinegrape's blood !
    Ah honey flood
  Through heart and senses pouring !

LXXXVII.

— Ah growing love from day to day
Better and better, with ne'er a stay !
    Ah sweet, sweet lay,
  Through ears to hearts resounding !
—Ah to hearts longing Thou quiet nook !
Ah roof for all, the world forsook !
    Ah tinkling brook
  For hearts with thirst abounding !
— Ah well-shaped mouth, ah comely face !
  Ah hawk-eye of pure splendor !
Ah love our loving souls always !
Thou woundest with Thy love's bright rays
    Our very grace :
  So sweet Thy love and tender !

LXXXVIII.

— Ah lustrous star, ah burning moon !
Ah shining sun of full-grown noon
    Both late and soon !
  Ah blooming heath's rich treasure !
— Ah eye's sweet fullness, ah heart's full food !
Ah love, where love has never trod !
    Ah love of God !
  Ah glorious eye-pleasure !

— Ah love Thou there, ah love Thou here !
 Ah love in every manner !
Ah love than which no love more dear
In heart of man its growth can rear !
   Heart of man ne'er
   Had sweeter love-enchainer !

LXXXIX.

—Ah well to-day and once more well !
Grief never in Thy heart did dwell ;
   Thou art a spell
   E'er growing with rapture richer !
— Ah sugar sweet, ah honey taste !
Ah of all things most pure and chaste,
   Ah good and blest !
Ah of our race best teacher !
Ah pure is he, ah pure is she,
   Ah bliss will never sever
From those, sweet love-branch, that love Thee !
Ah all that revel in Thy glee,
   Ah, they are free
From the grasp of hell forever !

XC.

— Ah glad to-day and once more glad !
Ah heart by lasting rapture fed,
   That never fled,
And stays with all in common !
— Ah good to-day, and once more good
And ever good, so pure a mood
   Holds Thy sweet blood
   And body, born of woman.

— Ah sweet love-wonder without a sword,
  Ah without fire a burning!
Happy who courts wounds from Thee, lord
To him the choicest thou'lt accord,
    That life doth hoard:
  Or moveth human yearning.

XCI.

— Ah Thou reward of all work done!
In sorrow Thou joy-pregnant tone!
    Ah tree upgrown,
  That with grace for all bloometh!
— Ah teller of all labor's care,
That man through Thee bore anywhere!
    Ah mild and fair!
  Who all grief overcometh.
Ah wise man, that dost ne'er forget
  Who honors to Thee render!
Ah King, who always made it fate
That good grow good and bad raise hate!
    Ah mirror-plate
  Of purest doctrine's splendor!

XCII.

Ah virtue pure, ah purest vase!
Ah of chaste eyes Thou mirror-glass!
    Ah adamas
  With fruitful virtues glowing!
— Ah festive day to pleasure lent!
Ah rapture without discontent!
    Ah sweet musk-scent!
  Ah flower gayly blowing!

— Ah heavenly kingdom where Thou art,
On earth, in hell, or heaven!
Ah cunning o'er all cunning's art!
Ah Thou, that knoweth every part!
    Ah sweet Christ's heart!
Ah sweetness without leaven!

XCIII.

Ah virtue there, ah virtue here!
Ah virtue on many a dark and drear
    Path, far and near!
Ah virtue e'er befriending!
Ah Thou self-conscious purity!
Ah goodness, those that cling to Thee
    So many be
Their number has no ending.
Ah father, mother, thou, and son!
    Ah brother both and sister!
Ah strong of faith as Jacob's son!
Ah King of earth's and heaven's throne!
    Ah Thou alone
Our friend to-day as yester!

CHAPTER IV.

from the meadow of the bird

WALTHER VON DER VOGELWEIDE.

ERY little is known positively of Walther's life, birthplace, and circumstances. That he was of noble birth appears conclusively from the contemporary testimony of other poets. That he was very poor, he himself repeatedly informs us ; and even his name, " Bird's pasture," indicates the very limited extent of the landed estate that may or may not have belonged to his family. But whether he was a native of the main-countries, or whether, as Franz Pfeiffer, the late editor of a new edition of his poems, seems to believe now, he was a Tyrolian, is still a matter of doubt. Wherever his birthplace was, he must have left home early,— about 1190,— and being very poor, gone to Austria for the purpose of cultivating himself in the art of a *Minnesinger.* He was then about twenty years of age, and probably enjoyed to the fullest extent the pleasures and delights of the always gay imperial city, where a period of peace and justice under the rule of the Hohenstauffens had developed a general prosperity, which that house and the closely related art-loving house of the Babenbergian Dukes liberally turned to the cultivation and protection of poetry, art, and science. Walther's songs of this time fairly flow over with expressions of enjoyment, and are easily recognized by the fresh grace of their musical movement as well as by the cheeriness of their tone. His teacher in the art of Minnesong-composition was undoubtedly Reinmar the Old, one of the foremost of Minnesinger. Under the tuition of this accomplished master, Walther soon perfected himself in his art, and became quite a favorite of the Babenbergian Duke Frederic I., the patron of poets, and indeed all manner of artists. Walther's external circumstances may therefore be supposed to have been, for a while at least, quite easy. A few of his Minnelieder, evidently composed at that time, will show the skill he had attained in his art, and the relish with which he enjoyed life and youth. The one " Under the Linden," particularly, has been admired for its wondrous melody in the original, and the grace of its naïve simplicity.

THE DREAM OF LOVE.

—" Take, lady, take this wreath ! "
Thus I spoke unto a fair and comely maiden.
—" And on the dance thou'lt breathe
Beauty by the flowers wherewith thy hair is laden.
— Had I but jewels of rare splendor,
    They should crown thee all, love !
    Trust my truthful soul, love ;
Take the word that I thee tender.

—" Thou art so comely made,
O, it makes me glad to give my wreath to thee.
—'Twas the best I had :
White and red flowers, I know where they found ma
    be ;

— They stand in yonder outstretched meadow.
    Where they're sweetly clinging,
    And the birds are singing,
There we'll pluck them in the shadow."

— She took that which I had
Altogether like a child that feeleth shame.
  — Her cheeks turned all o'er red,
As by the lily glows the rose upon her stem.
    — Ashamed her bright eyes 'gan to flutter ;
     Yet her head she bended,
     Thus me thanks she spended ;
What I else got, ne'er I'll utter.

  — I thought that all life's hours
Never had upon me flung such happiness.
  — The flowers fell in showers
From the trees adown to us upon the grass.
    — Look then in laughter I 'gan breaken,
     Being so drowned in pleasure
     With my dream's sweet treasure :
Then day broke and I must waken.

  — This is the cause that I
All this summer, wheresoe'er I see a maid,
  — Into her eyen must spy —
Perhaps it *is* she ; then were all my grief allayed.
    — Who knows ? this dance now may enfold her.
     Ladies, pity on it !
     Each lift up her bonnet !
Ah, could I wreath-crowned behold her !
  9

UNDER THE LINDEN.

— Under the linden,
        On the meadow,
Where our bed arrangèd was,
    — There now you may find ee'n
        In the shadow
Broken flowers and crushèd grass.
— Near the woods, down in the vale,
        Tandaradi!
Sweetly sang the nightingale.

    — I poor begrieved me
        Came to the prairie:
Look, my lover'd gone before.
    — There he received me —
        Gracious Mary! —
That now with bliss I'm brimming o'er,
— Kissed he me?   Ah, thousand hours!
        Tandaradi!
See, my mouth, how red it flowers!

    — There 'gan he making,
        O, so cheery!
From flowers a bed-place rich outspread.
    — At which outbreaking
        In laughter merry
You'll find whoe'er the path does tread.
— By the roses he can see,
        Tandaradi!
Where my head lay cozily.

— How he caressed me—
Knew't one ever,
God defend ! ashamed I should be.
— Whereto he pressed me,
No, no, never
Shall any know't but him and me
And a birdlet in the tree ;
Tandaradi !
Sure we can trust it, cannot we ?

ECSTASY OF LOVE.

— I am now so full of joy,
That into any folly I might throw me ;
— For there 's a chance that I
Can win my lady signs of love to show me.
— Look ! thus rise my hopes and blow me
Far higher than the sunshine floats ; — be
gracious, maid, unto me !

— Ne'er I on the fair one glanced
But with love's glow my eyes 'gan sparkle clearer.
— This always to me chanced :
And e'en cold winter to my heart grew dearer.
— Others deemed't a churlish cheever,
What time to me it seemed as if May had
indeed drawn nearer.

— This most pleasant song I've sung
In honor of my lady, and unchary.
— She must thank me for't ere long,
Then for her sake will I be ever merry.

— Though she wound my heart unwary :
What of it ? whether't hurteth me ?   It may
do the contrary.

— No one may so far succeed,
To part me ever from the love I bear her.
— If I turned from her indeed,
Then where should I find maiden nobler, dearer,
— One more guileless, *debonnairer ?*
Than Helen or Diana she is better famed
and fairer.

WOMEN AND SPRING.

— When the flowers from out the grass 'gin spring-
ing,
As if towards the sparkling sunshine smiling
On a May-day in morn's early glow :
— And the birdlets in their best are singing,
With delight the flow'ry world beguiling :
O, what rapture can compare thereto ?
— It surely is quite half a heaven !
If you ask what better could be given,
I'll tell you quickly what amain
My eye has gladdened and would gladen still could
I see it again.

— When a noble, pure, and lovely lady
Well arrayed, her hair all tied up brightly,
For pastime goes to some social place ;
— Courteous-mannered, with companions, ready,
To look back she turns at times, but slightly :

As the sun shines forth from star-set ways.
— Let May bring all its freshest glow us,
Where such pleasant wonder can it show us
As by her body there's displayed?
We all turn from the flowers to go and gaze upon
    the noble maid.

— Well, then, if ye'd see the truth, I'll summon
At May's festival ye all to gather,
    For he's come with all his powers and art.
— Look on him and look on worthy women,
And then judge which outranks which, and whether
    I have not made mine the better part.
— Ah me, were ordered I to choose then
Which for th' other one I'd rather loose, then!
How quick should my decision prove!
Sir May, I'd liken you to March, before I'd loose
    my lady-love.

The following poems belong to a maturer period of
Walther's life, as will appear both by their form and
contents. They have been selected, not only with a
view to illustrate the chief of the Minnesinger himself,
but also as conveying in their different forms and
contents the best notion of the general range of Minnesong. In the second poem the last line has twelve
feet, divided into two parts of six each. In the third
poem the mentioning of the loved one's name as Hildegunde excites astonishment, as it was considered
utterly unknightly and unminstrel-like by both the
German and the Provençal troubadour, ever to mention the name of the loved lady. Walther himself in
other poems complains about the rabble who pester

him to tell his sweetheart's name. Mr. Pfeiffer's suggestion, that the name of Hildegunde, occurring in this poem, refers to the Hildegunde of the old German legend "Walther and Hildegunde," and was used by our Walther for the very purpose of chastising the spiers after his lady-love's name, by giving his lady the legendary representative name of constant love, seems not so very farfetched. The lengthening of the last strophe by a refrain, occurs also in other *Minnelieder*. The cuckoo's cry, alluded to in the second strophe, presages in superstitious lore a year of starvation, if you hear it before having broken fast in the morning ; but the meaning of the ass's bray, heard under like circumstances, has not been ascertained as yet. Undoubtedly it was quite as serious and fearful a curse as the cuckoo's cry. Concerning the poem to Steadiness, it may be of interest to remark that this *personifying* of virtues and vices was a peculiarity of the Minnesinger, and was carried by them to an extreme length.

THE COQUETTE.

— Long in silence to remain I'd thought ;
Now must I sing, howe'er as erst.
— Hereunto good people me have brought,
Who well in all command me durst ;
— I must sing and I must say,
And what they like that I must do. — Well, then
my lament swell must they.

— Hear the wonder which to me did chance,
As my reward for all I've done.

— There 's a woman will not on me glance
    For whom I that renown have won,
— Which so proudly moves her soul !
Does she not know if I leave singing — that then
      her praise
        will vanish all ?

— God ! what curses down on her would rain,
    If I should stop my singing now.
— All who praise her now, I know, would then
    Abuse her without me ; for, trow,
— Thousand hearts did gladsome grow
When she was gracious ; who will blame her — if I
      from her
        must part me so.

— When I yet believed that she was good,
    Who then more kind to her than I ?
— Now 'tis at an end ; let then her mood
    Turn as it will, she may rely,
— If with love she makes me glad
Her life will by my life be honored — but kills she
      me then is she dead.

— Must I in her service e'en grow old,
    The while she surely grows not young,
— Lo, perhaps my hair so gray will mould,
    She'll wish to choose the young among.
— S'help you God, young gentleman,
Revenge me and her withered skin — with fresh
      grown twigs
        teach manners then !

LOVE IS TWO HEARTS' BLESSED RAPTURE

— What is love? will some one tell me?
If I know't a part I'd like to know it more.
   — Now who knows it rightly, hail me
And expound me this: how makes love hearts so
      sore?
   — Love is Love, when she does well,
Does she woe, then is she not called rightly Love;
      nor —
   do I know how then her name I ought to spell.

   — If my guess does rightly capture
Love's true meaning, I would have you tell me:
      Yea,
   — Love is two hearts' blessed rapture!
If't they equally divide, love theirs must be.
   — But if they divide it not,
One heart ne'er alone can hold love's blessèd rap-
      ture —
   Lady, O do thou help me to bear my lot!

   — Sweet, for me, if thou me eas'st not,
This load weighs too sore; wouldst help, help now
      and right.
   — Car'st thou, though, for me the least not,
Then speak out at last, and I give up the fight,
   — And a free man stay always.
One thing though thou shouldst remember, that thee
      rightly — no
   one mickle better than myself can praise.

— Can my love pay sweet with sour?
Thinketh she I'll give her love in change for woe?
— Shall I glorify her power,
That she turn it to make me seem e'en more low?
— Then did I most badly spy!
But what chatter I poor earless, eyeless wretch yet?
    — He
whom love has blinded has to see no eye.

HILDEGUNDE.

— Those who in the winter me my joy have taken,
  Or women they or men they were,
— May this summer-time their pleasure them not
      slacken,—
  But why swear I not curses rare?
— Too few I know, and not one fitter
Than the evil word: O damn them!— no, no! that
    were all too bitter.

— Yet two very hearty curses know I sheer,
  That curse e'en as my will is bent,
— May they ever hear the ass and cuckoo ere
  Their morning's meal they come anent!
Then, poor wretches, woe 's your ditty!
Knew I that they would repent them — I'd, for God!
    on them take pity.

— One should patience to unpatience ever show,
  This to the shameless bringeth shame;
— Whom the wicked hate unjustly, they do so
  By reason of his virtue's claim.

— If the loved one would but cheer me,
Who so well might cheer my sorrow, — little for
    their hate I'd care me.

— I'll to all the world upon her body swear,
    This oath let her well mark and ponder !
— Hold I any one, woman or maid, more dear,
    Then hell my soul may swallow yonder.
— Now, if kin ness in her dwelleth,
She will trust this oath of mine — and
        still the grief that my heart swelleth.

— Gentlemen and friends, now lend betimes your
    aid ;
    The end is nigh, for things stand so :
— If in this love battle I'm not victor made,
    Joy ne'er again will in me glow.
— My heart, cleft by love asunder,
Must forever open stay, — unless her kisses do the
    wonder ;
My heart, cleft by love asunder,
Must forever open stay, — unless love heals it o'er
    and under ;
My heart, cleft by love asunder,
Must forever open stay, — unless 'tis healt by
    Hildegunde.

THE ENEMIES OF LOVE.

— Us all at present — the same grace stands much
    in need :
That to genuine gladness we again should turn.
— A sight unpleasant — has laid all my gladness
    dead :
That the young so grimly now joy seem to spurn.
— Their young life, what good is't them ?
True gladness they should with it gather.
Aye, would they but in gladness bathe e'er !
Then, young men, you women's help might claim.

— Now am I brimming — glad and must with glad-
    ness glow
Through the dear one, what meanwhile me may
    betide.
— Here am I seeming — yet still with her my heart
    does go,
So that often people me as senseless chide.
— Should they e'er together join :
My heart, my body, — with both's full forces :
Aye, soon would feel my new resources,
They that blocked my joys, those enemies mine !

— These watchers prying — always us't enjoy pre-
    vent :
For their watch has many worthy a love dismayed.
'T keeps sorely trying — me ; when her I come anent,
Then must I avoid her, the most blessed maid !
— Still that time I trust to liven,
When she a tryst shall give, where neither

Shall feel the watch — O thus together,
Then would mickle love to me be given.

— Full many a one pryeth — of my love and who she
  be,
  Whom I serve and always have served hitherto.
— Now this annoyeth — me ; and so I answer: "Three
  Do I serve, and for a fourth one hope I grow."
— Yet she only know'st, I ween,
  Who heart from body me expelleth,
  Who wounded well, and eke well healeth,
Whom o'er all I ought to serve: my Queen.

— O love, dear lady — go and seize her lovingly,
  Who me has swayed and so completely holds in
    sway ;
— Teach her how ready — love's sway may estab-
    lished be,
  Perhaps she loving love will also learn t'obey.
— Then she also will believe
  With all my heart I love her truly.
  O love confirm her this faithfully ;
And her service gladly I'll achieve.

STEADINESS.

— Mistress Steady 's my dismay ;
I know not if she brings praise,
But I know she works sore grief.
— Since love held me under sway
Bidding me go Steady's ways,
I did ne'er from grief retrieve.

— Let me go, my dearest Mistress Steady!
 For howe'er I press my lady
 She 's steadier in refusing me;
— My too great steadiness will prove my ruin—
  unless love wounds her equally.

 — Who would ever praise the man
 Whom this steadiness brings joy,
 If he Steady's paths pursues?
 — But, who ne'er did aught attain
 From her, and yet stays her by:
 Look, his steadiness pleases us.
— Thus have I, e'en, wooed this Mistress Steady,
 And yet nothing happened ready.
 This change thou, blessèd lady-love!
— That I the butt of her, the false and faithless,—
  of steadiness no more may prove.

 — Had I not of joy my part
 Built upon thee, dear heart's love,
 Some way out of 't could be shown.
 — But since all my weal thou art,
 And my joy and worth e'er throve
 And still rests in thee alone:
— Should I now my heart tear from thee, dearest,
 I'd but hurt myself the nearest.
 This surely were not wisely done.
— Yet shouldst thou, blessèd woman, keep in mind
  — how long I've grieved for thee alone.

 — Lady, I know well thy mood;
 That thou steady lov'st to be

I've discovered long ago.
— For thee ever yet kept good
Woman's cunning's purity,
Which all women holdeth so.
— Thus thy bliss and honor do I cherish,
I've no other joy to nourish:
Now speak, is this reward enough?
— Thou shouldst, O lady, let me that enjoy — which
    I so long have longed for, love!

But the death of the German Emperor Henry VI.,
which occurred September 28, 1197, put a stop to
Walther's quiet and cheerful minstrel life, as it also
ended the previous peace and quiet of the whole German country. Pope Innocent III. refused to recognize Henry's minor son, Frederic II., whom the
Germans had elected; and Philip of Swabia, the
child's uncle and a son of Barbarossa, and Otto of
Bavaria, arose as rival candidates for the throne.
The whole empire fell a prey to confusion, war, and
party dispute; and Walther, a thoughtful and deep-
feeling observer of affairs, took henceforth active
part in the politics of the day. His patron, Duke
Frederic, having also died, and Leopold, Frederic's
successor, having proved rather unfriendly to Walther, the poet, after having in vain tried to obtain
the patronage of the famous Landgrave of Thüringen,
left Vienna for the court of Philip of Swabia, for
whom he had declared his preference at the outset in
the following Sayings or *Sprüche:* —

I.

— Upon a stone, moss-sheeted,
Cross-leggèd I was seated;
My arms upon my knees did rest,
Whilst in my hands, as in a nest,
Both chin and cheeks lay nicely.
Then pondered I how wisely
We in this world might move and live.
Yet could my mind no counsel give
— How we three things might gather
And yet of them lose neither.
The two are honor and worldly good;
Either the other doth preclude.
The third 's God's grace all-shielding,
Both others over-gilding.
These would I in my heart compel!
But alas! 'tis impossible,
— That worldly good and favor
With God's great grace should ever
Into the same one heart be taken.
Path and ways have them forsaken,
For untruth lies in waiting,
Force on the streets keeps prating,
And peace and right are deeply gored.
The three can have no safe protection till peace and
right are quite restored.

II.

— I heard a water skimming,
And saw the fishes swimming;

I saw what in the world there was :
Fields and woods, leaves, reeds, and grass.
What crawleth and ascendeth,
And feet to th' earth downbendeth.
This saw I, and I tell you that
None of these all live without hate.
— The beasts, and e'en the crawling
Worms e'er are fighting and bawling.
Thus e'en the birds do. Still I see
That in one thing they do agree —
They'd hold themselves destroyèd,
Lest they one court employèd.
Hence king and law they choose by a word,
And order servant man and lord.
— Ah woe thee, German nation !
How great thy degradation !
The very fly her king doth own ;
And lo ! thine honor goeth down !
Repent thee, O repent thee !
Thy selfish princes rent thee !
Too many kings press thee, alack !
O Philip, take the emperor's crown, and tell the
others to stand back !

Walther seems to have had a sincere liking for
Philip, whose praise, indeed, is sounded by all his
contemporaries, and whose coronation at Mayence in
the fall of 1198, Walther has celebrated in the following neat Saying : —

— The crown is older far than good King Philip is ;
There you all may see a wonder ; even this : —

How could the smith have made it him so fitting?
— His fine imperial head becometh it so well,
That no one now can break or separate the spell;
  Neither detracts, but each gives th' other greeting.
— Aye, both each on each other glow,
The precious jewel on the young sweet man sits so,
  That this eye-pleasure proudly greet our princes.
If one yet doubts who 's lord and king,
Let him behold the Orphan in the crown's gold ring !
  That precious stone our princes' choice evinces.

The Orphan was the name of the most precious jewel in the German imperial crown, and was so called from the fact of being unequaled in value and size by any other precious stone. Otto, the rival of Philip, and the favorite of the Pope, had been crowned with false crown jewels on July the fourteenth of the same year at Aachen ; but the fact that Philip was crowned with the genuine jewels, secured to him the sympathy of the majority of the German princes, and explains the allusions in the above poem.

The two coronations gave rise to a civil war and disturbances, that were fanned by all the power of Rome. These occasioned the following Saying : —

III.

  — My eyes saw men and women
  Hold stealthy speech in common ;
  Then did I hear and did I see
  What all the world did secretly.
  — At Rome I heard them lying,
  Two kings to quarrel inspiring.
  10

Therefrom the worst war 'rose and raged,
That ever man at any time waged ;
— Dividing into factions
The priests' and the laymen's sections.
It was a dread above all dread ;
Both soul and body then lay dead.
The priests fought e'en like gay men,
But there were more of laymen.
Then laid they down their swords disgusted,
And 'gain used priestly arms, more trusted.
They banned e'en whom they wot to,
And not him whom they ought to.
Then felt God's dwellings their dread spell.
I heard from far off in a cell
Great wailing my way straying :
A cloister-monk was praying ;
To God he uttered his soul's gloom :
"Alas, the Pope is far too young — O Lord, help
    Thou Thy Christendom ! "

In the following years of political troubles Walther seems to have been untiringly active in the cause which he conceived to be the right one. Nor were his Sayings without influence, — an influence that seems to have been extended from Vienna to Rome ; for when Walther, in 1213, issued one of them against the *truncos* which Pope Innocent had ordered to be put up in all Catholic churches for contributions, ostensibly in support of the Crusades, we find it alluded to by Thomasin of Zercläre, as a most grievous sin against his holiness, and as a Saying which had kept thousands from giving their contributions to the holy cause. Walther of course had looked upon the matter as merely a device to fill the Pope's own coffers with foreign money.

When Philip, in 1204–5, overcame his rival Otto, and was crowned again in Aachen, Walther's political activity seems to have discontinued ; and neither Philip's subsequent assassination, in 1208, nor Otto's later unanimous accession to the imperial crown, in 1209, are alluded to by him. It was not till Otto, in 1210, was excommunicated by the Pope, that Walther again brought his poetical services into the political field, taking strong side against papal interference with German political affairs. Meantime we find him roaming in true minstrel knight fashion over the country : now with the Duke of Kärnten, who has a Saying or two thrown at his head for withholding a promised suit of new clothes from Walther ; now with Duke Leopold of Austria, brother of the poet's first patron ; and now in the princely Abbey Tegernsee, famed for its learning and hospitality, but dealing out to Walther but a very cool reception, as the following Saying testifies : —

— They told me much of Tegernsee :
  How great its hospitality.
Then turned I more than one mile from the highway.
  — Truly I am a curious man,
  That I myself so little plan
And far too much let other people dictate my way,
— I'll scold them not ; God bless and make us
  better!

> They gave me water.
> Thus, foolish plotter,
> I turned from the Monk's table simply wetter.

He also went again to the art-loving court of Thüringen, and this time met with better success than at the first attempt. The mention of Walther's name in the poem of the "Wartburg Minstrel's War," is undoubtedly owing to this stay at the court, where the most famous of German poets had congregated during the turmoil of the times.

In this manner, now roving from one court to another, now in Vienna with the Emperor or Duke Leopold, Walther passed two or three years, fighting hard for the Emperor's cause, and in spite of repeated insults and humiliations from the obstinate, changeable Otto, remaining a faithful friend to the recognized representative of the German nation; inciting him to virtuous actions and frankly censuring his faults both in poems and in private converse. But when Otto in the conflicts of his reign was finally defeated altogether at Bouvines in July 1212, Walther, who had followed his flight to Cologne, and who was one of the last friends to leave him, turned also to the legitimate successor, Frederic II., who intrusted him with the education of his son, the subsequent Emperor Henry VII., probably on recommendation of the Archbishop of Cologne, who had learned to recognize Walther's worth during his short stay there with the hiding Emperor. Walther's little scholar seems to have given him much trouble. He also has a Saying thrown at his head for his stupidity, but was likewise the occasion of the following: —

Children with rod ruling —
'Tis the worst of schooling.
Who is honor made to know
Him a word seems as a blow.
Him a word seems as a blow
Who is honor made to know.
'Tis the worst of schooling :
Children with rod ruling.

Guard your tongues 'gainst leaking ;
To you young I'm speaking !
Put a bolt before the door,
Let no evil word get o'er !
Let no evil word get o'er,
Put a bolt before the door !
To you young I'm speaking,
Guard your tongues 'gainst leaking !

Guard your eyes, moreover,
Free or under cover !
On the good reflecting aye,
Turn their glance from evil's way.
Turn their glance from evil's way
On the good reflecting aye,
Free or under cover,
Guard your eyes, moreover !

Guard your ears securely,
They will fool you surely :
If you evil words let in
It dishonors all within.
It dishonors all within
If you evil words let in.

They will fool you surely :
Guard your ears securely.

Guard the three forever,
'Gainst too free behavior.
Tongue, eyes, ears, are all inclined
To badness, and to evil blind.
To badness, and to evil blind
Tongue, eyes, ears, are all inclined.
'Gainst too free behavior,
Guard the three forever !

The felicitous form of this little poem, each strophe
being written so that it may be read from the first
line downwards or from the last line upwards, fit it
admirably to the mind of children ; and the instructions it conveys are certainly signs that the poet com-
prehended the position of an educator.

But Walther soon gave up the tutorship of the
young Crown Prince. He continued, however, to
stay at the court of the Emperor Frederic II., an admired poet and esteemed counselor. The Emperor,
a noble-minded man, received the censure of his
friend with the same graciousness as his praise, and
after a while gratified the highest wish of the poet
by conferring upon him the rental of some estate, a
small enough affair, probably not more than two
hundred dollars per annum, if so much, but sufficient
for the poet, who only wanted to be sure that the last
days of his life might be passed without actual suffering for food and clothes. Walther also received presents from other courts to which he paid visits ; and

one of his verses commemorates the gift of a diamond from a prince of Katzenellenbogen.

In the year 1228 Walther followed the Crusade of his Emperor, and had his wish gratified to behold the land where his Saviour had lived and suffered. Either in his travels to or home from Palestine, he made that visit to his native home, which is so touchingly commemorated in his "Lament."

Nothing is known of his life since that return. He died, probably, about 1230, in Wurzburg, near which he had likely enough passed the last year or years of his life, upon the estate conferred upon him by the Emperor; and the heart that in life "had never enjoyed but a half day's uninterrupted joy," as he confesses himself, found peace at last in death. Of his relation to women we know nothing but what can be gleaned from his poems.

The following poems are from his later age, as their melancholy tone clearly enough expresses. The first one about the "Lazy Angels" shows that even at that time the notion that angels might be better employed than in "loafing around the throne," — namely, by aiding the Crusaders, — was not foreign from men's minds. The last and most beautiful of all Walther's poems fittingly closes the list.

THE LAZY ANGELS.

I.

He who beginning ne'er acquired
And who beginning first inspired,
Can will make end and also without-end.
Hence, as all this rests in his own hand,

Who deserves our praise with equal worth?
He be the first one in my measures;
His all other praise o'er treasures:
　　The praise is blessed He claims on earth.

II.

Now praise we also the maiden dear,
To whom her son refuses ne'er.
She is his mother, who from hell us saved.
Comfort, by us o'er all comforts craved,
　　Is't to know her will in heaven is wooed.
Up, then, ye old and young, keep ringing
Loud her praise, her glory singing:
　　'Tis good to praise her, for she's good.

III.

Ye angels, too, my praise might cull
But that I am not a fool so dull.
Why wrought ye yet the heathens no distraction?
Since then no one sees or hears your action,
　　Say, what have ye in the good cause done?
Could I, like you, help God by willing,
Then indulged I no appealing;
　　I'd leave you, gentlemen, alone.

IV.

Sir Michael, Sir Gabriel,
Sir Devil's enemy, Raphael,
Ye practice wisdom, strength, and medicine.
Three great choirs of angels too, I ween,

Have you ready to obey your word.
Would ye my praise? Show sense, don't sneak back,
Help to find the heathen's weak back:
　To praise ye now would be absurd.

MY CRITICS.

— The bilious doubters say, that now all things lie
　　dead,
　That no one any more is singing;
— But sure they ought to take in mind the general
　　dread:
　How all the world with strife is ringing!
— Comes happy time you'll hear again us sing and
　　say,
　　　To cause you wonder.
I heard a little bird say just in the same way, —
　　　'Twas nestling yonder:
" I shall not sing till break of day."

— Bad men have to good women sore traduced my
　　song,
　And said their name't had scandalous rendered;
— Well, let them all combine, they'll hear of me ere
　　long;
　A coward he, who skulks when slandered.
— Did ever one of German women sing more true?
　　　Sure, I did sever
The good ones from the bad; and this their hate
　　first drew.
　　　Sang I their favor
In equal terms, how would that do?

— Envy and hate ! for one thing I'm obliged to you
  When you as messengers are entered,
— That you so dearly love the good men to pursue ;
  Thus shame upon your master 's centered.
— You spies, since you no steadfast man could e'er
  decoy,
      — He'd curse you sooner, —
Return to your own house ; it cannot fail, your lie
      Must bring dishonor
To lying mouth and cross-grained eye.

In the legendary lore of Walther's time the Devil
kept a tavern called World, the hostess of which was
most beautiful when beheld in front, but of hideous
aspect when seen from behind. In this poem Walther has a dialogue with the lady, a form of poetry
very frequent with the Minnesinger : —

GOOD-NIGHT TO MINE HOSTESS WORLD.

— Dear World, thou shouldst thy host let know
  That I have paid him quite enough,
— My great debt now is settled, so
  He from my bond should strike it off.
— Who owes him aught, may well feel sorrow ;
Rather than stay long in his debt, I would go to a
  Jew and borrow.
He holds off silent till the day,
Then he straightway a pawn demands, if the poor
  debtor cannot pay.

— " Walther, thou worriest without need,
  I want thee to remain with me.

—Think, how I gave thee honor's meed,
  How often thy will I humored thee,
What time thou did'st implore me rarely.
It gave me often great concern, that thou did'st this
      so very sparely;
  Consider't well, thy life is pleasant,
If thou dost really quarrel with me, thou'lt ne'er be
      happy as at present."

— Dear World, thy breast too long I've suckled,
  I now will wean me, it is time;
— Thy soft caresses tight me buckled,
  Their pleasures with my heart did chime.
— Yea, when I looked in th' eye thee clearly,
Thy features beamed most gloriously; this must I
      say: the truth 'tis merely.
  Yet all too great was thy disgrace
When I at last thy back beheld; now must I ever
      hold thee base.

— " Since then I cannot turn thee back,
  At least do one thing I request:
— On many a bright passed day thought take,
  And do at times thy glances cast
— On me when time on you hangs heavy."
This would I do with greatest pleasure, but that I
      fear a hidden levy
  From thee, 'gainst which no guard could keep.
God give thee, Lady, a good-night; I'll go meanwhile
      to bed and sleep.

The following poem was probably written on Walther's travels in the Crusade of 1228. The last lines

evidently allude to some then pending negotiations for
a cessation of hostilities. The longing for the bounding billows refers to the sea voyage, which would take
them to Palestine : —

CRUSADER'S HYMN.

— Sweet love of Holy Spirit,
Direct sick mind and steer it !
God, who the first didst rear it,
    Protect Thou Christendom !
— Art lies of pleasure barren,
No rose blooms more in Sharon ;
Comfort of all th' ill-starren,
    O, help dispel this gloom !
— Keep, Saviour, from all ill us !
We long for the bounding billows,
Thy Spirit's love must thrill us,
    Repentant heart's true friend.
Thy blood for us thou'st given,
Unlocked the gates of heaven ;
Now strive we as we've striven
    To gain the blessèd land.
Our wealth and blood grows thinner :
God yet shall make us winner
'Gainst him, who many a sinner
    Holds pawnèd in his hand.

— This short life speed of wind hath,
Death us still sinful findeth,
He who to God him bindeth,
    May yet escape from hell.

— With grief rare grace was mated,
Christ's wounds heal unabated ;
His land must liberated
   Be quickly without fail.
— O queen above all women !
Show lasting help unto men !
Thy child there got its summon
   And human life did quaff.
— His spirit o'er us running,
Teach us the heathen's cunning !
Unchristians ! see them shunning
   With fear the judge's staff,
Which Jews too sorely flayeth !
Loud cries each tribe and prayeth.
Glory the cross arrayeth :
   O haste we to the grave !

— We must lay off what 's earthy,
Would we his boon be worthy.
For us death bore as birth he ;
   His comfort us is spared :
— His cross, blessed by each nation,
Has wrought mankind's salvation.
Who turns from doubt's mutation,
   His soul with him has paired.
— Ah thoughtless body, treasured,
Thy years have all been measured,
Death took us, as we leisured,
   Us sinners doomed and lost.
Now let us all quick hasten
Where we secure may fasten
The heavenly kingdom's crest on
   Our zealous soul ; we must :

God with a hero's power
Will there his foes make cower.
Crowd then from field and tower
    Knights of the Holy Ghost !

— God, keep Thy help us sending !
With Thy right hand aid-lending,
Protect us till the ending,
    When't last our soul us leaves,
— From hell's fires flaming clamor,
Lest we fall 'neath the hammer !
Too oft we've heard with tremor,
    How pitiably it grieves
— The land so pure and holy
All helpless, and fearfully !
Jerusalem, weep lowly,
    That thou forgotten art !
The heathen's boastful glory
Put thee in slav'ry hoary,
Christ, by Thy name's proud story,
    In mercy take her part !
And help those, sorely shaken,
Who treaties there would maken,
That we may not be taken
    And conquered at the start !

LAMENT.

— Ah me! whither have vanished — all my years and
  youth?
Has life been then but dreamèd — or is't all a truth?
And was that really somewhat — which I lived and
  thought?
Surely I must have slumbered — though I knew it not.
— Now I am awakened — yet is to me unknown
What once I knew as one hand — knoweth the other
  one.
The country and the people — 'mongst whom my life
  passed by
From childhood, are estrangèd — as if 'twere all a
  lie.
— They who were once my playmates — weary've
  grown and old,
The meadows have been broken — the woods cut
  down and sold.
If yonder river flowed not — as it once did flow,
I do believe this weary — despair would lay me low.
Me greet with hesitation — many who knew me well.
This wretched world is everywhere — a most wretchèd
  hell ;
And then I think of many — days of light and joy,
That now e'en as a stroke on the sea — have gone
  forever by,
  Forever more ; ah me !

— Ah me, how sad and careworn — young men now
  appear !
The men, who once would never — allow grief to draw
  near,

Do nothing now but weary.— Ah me, how can it be?

Where in the world I turn me — none seem glad to
    me.

— Dancing, laughing, singing— grim care has driv'n
    away.

No Christian man saw e'er — so miserable a day.

Behold how e'en our women — walk with strange
    head gear ;

And how proud knights and nobles — clownish wrap-
    pings wear,

— Letters disapproving — Rome has sent our way.

To mourn we have permission — no more to be gay.

It grieves me to my heart's core — we once did live
    so grand !

That now from joyous laughing — to weeping I must
    bend.

The wild birds of the woods — grow sad at our com-
    plaint :

What wonder is't that I — from sheer despair turn
    faint?

But what?   O wretched me ! — have I been led to
    scoff?

Who follows earthly happiness — from heaven's bliss
    turneth off
           For evermore ; ah me !

— Ah me, how we are poisoned — with the sweetness
    of the earth !

I see the bitterest gall flow — from sweetest honey
    forth.

The world is outward beautiful — white, green, and
    red,

But inward, O, a sombre black, — gloomy, dark, and
 dead.

— Yet now to who have listened — a comfort I will
 show :

Even a gentle penance — forgiveness shall bestow.

Remember this, O knightly lords, — 'tis yours to
 hear th' appeal :

You bear the glittering helmets — and breastplates of
 strong steel,

— Moreo'er the shields so steady — and consecrated
 swords !

O God, were I worthy — to join the victor-lords !

Then should I like the others — achieve a prize untold :

Not lands, as have been promised, — nor the noble's
 gold,

But O, a wondrous crown — for evermore to wear,

Which e'en the poorest soldier — may win him with
 his spear ;

Yea, if that welcome crusade — I might follow o'er
 the sea,

I evermore should sing : All's well ! — and nevermore :
 Ah me !

   Nevermore ah me !

That Walther von der Vogelweide was held in the
highest esteem by the contemporary poets and writers
of that age we have manifold authority ; none weightier and more beautiful than that of Gottfried von
Strassburg in that celebrated passage of " Tristan and
Isolde," where he singles out Walther as the leader of
all the Minnesinger-nightingales. But more lovely

11

even than as a poet and great artist does Walther appear as a man; this even the few of his poems here given, and the short sketch of his life, must make apparent. He was evidently from early age an earnest observer of human affairs in all its relations and phases; a thoughtful student and teacher; a sincere worshipper of the divine; an active member of the state; and in all things remarkably clear-sighted and unprejudiced; never a partisan so far as to stay blind to the good side of what he opposed. If as a tutor he had already abandoned the use of the rod, and learned to denounce it as the worst kind of schooling; as a politician he recognized whatever merits the opposite party held, and denounced any injustice and wrong made patent of his own; whilst in religion, opposition to the abuses of the Church was never separated from devout faith and adoration; a worship so pure and clear-minded that it could even shake off with a smile the imagery of lazily floating angels of paradise. Most deservedly have Walther's works grown popular again in Germany as they once were; for although his comprehensive mind was little tainted by the prejudices of nationality, he is, in his thorough earnestness and rare purity of spirit, even more truly a representative German than either Goethe or Schiller.

CHAPTER V.

ULRICH VON LICHTENSTEIN.

THE exact year of Ulrich's birth is not known; it was probably between 1200–1205. At the precocious age of five years, while his favorite amusement was galloping his hobby-horse in the castle court-yard, Ulrich listened eagerly to and treasured in his heart the sayings of his fellow wooden-horsemen, perhaps a year or two older than himself, to the effect that true honor and happiness could be acquired only by faithfully serving a noble and lovely woman, and loving her as one's own life. As the same sentiments were repeated to him from all sides, by old and young, and enounced not only in prose but still more impressively in *Minnelieder*, young Ulrich, at the age of twelve, thought it high time to take the first step toward the realization of this bliss. He chose for his lady-love a princess of Meran, whose page he became. A marvel of beauty and virtue, but rather too high of rank for Ulrich's aspirations, this paragon of all earthly women henceforth exercised a wondrous influence upon his life. His youthful passion exhausted itself in extravagant efforts to act and feel like a true knightly lover. He tells with ecstasy how happy he was when he saw her hand touch the flowers he had

gathered for her, when his own had touched them before, or when he could carry away the water wherein
at dinner-time she had dipped her fair hands, to drink
it with passionate enjoyment in his private room. For
full five years he thus served her with all the zeal of
a boyish lover. At the end of that time he was
placed with the Margrave Henry of Austria, to learn
from that chivalrous gentleman all the accomplishments of a true knight — fighting, riding, composing
sweet poems, singing, and serving the ladies. He
passed his apprenticeship and was admitted into
knighthood at the festival wherewith Leopold of Austria celebrated the wedding of his daughter Agnes
with a Duke of Saxony in 1223. At this occasion
were assembled some five thousand knights, and the
utmost profusion of enjoyable things attended the
festivities. Ulrich here saw his lady-love again, but,
for fear of observers, spoke not a word to her. Secretly he vowed, however, that henceforth all his
knighthood should be devoted to her ; in obedience
to which resolution he sallied forth, after the festivals
were ended, to roam over the country at large, and
fought victoriously at some twelve tourneys, for which
good luck he of course offered up silent thanks to
the lady of his heart.

During the winter, however, when the tourneys
had stopped and Ulrich had nothing to do but reflect, he thought it very hard that he should thus pas-
sionately worship a lady and she remain ignorant of
his adoration. In visiting a neighboring castle he
found in a niece of his a proper mediator between
himself and his lady-love, the noble princess. So he

sang a song in the lady's honor, which the niece undertook to communicate, and promised at the same time to sound the lady's heart as to its entertaining any passion for Ulrich. In the happiest state of mind Ulrich left his niece, and went in quest of adventures and other ladies for five weeks ; when returning, he learned the disagreeable news that the princess had found his song very neatly composed but his love altogether too high-flown ; and had suggested that even if she could forget her rank, the ugliness of his lips must estrange all women from him. It seems that Ulrich had a sort of double under-lip. No sooner had the knight heard this feature of his countenance condemned by his lady-love, than in spite of the entreaties of his niece to leave his mouth as God had made it, he bestrode his horse, and set out for Grätz to a surgeon, whom he requested to cut the third lip off. The surgeon advised him to defer the operation till next spring. Ulrich therefore passed the winter again in riding around visiting the ladies. In the spring he met a servant of his lady-love, whom he took along with him to the surgeon that he might witness the operation on his lip performed. Ulrich submitted to it with great courage, lay on a sick-bed for some six weeks before he was completely cured again, and sent word to his lady that he would gladly cut off his hand also if she should wish it. This she did not see fit to require ; and the account she had heard of his great courage in undergoing the painful operation, no less than a new song he had composed for her during his long illness, softened her heart so far that she consented to see him, the pretext being that she would like to see how he looked now.   So the love-sick knight, to whom all the troubles of life appeared as nought so long as life held out the hope that he might some time attain the possession of his loved one, hurried to the meeting, which occurred at a riding-party of noble knights and ladies.   Here the princess gave Ulrich fair opportunity to speak to her, but in a co-quettish sort of a way, which stopped his mouth, so that however much his heart said, " Now speak, now speak, now speak ! " his lips remained closed ; for which instance of stupidity in not understanding fem-inine ways the princess pulled out a lock of the poor knight's hair as he helped her to descend from the saddle, whispering that he evidently lacked that bold-ness for which he had been unjustly celebrated.   Ul-rich was in despair, and wanted to die ; but next day chancing to meet his fair one again, summoned up courage, and begged her to receive his love, and ac-cept him as her knight until death.   She maintained her coquettish way of keeping the knight fast in her bonds, so as to have all the glory of his service and yet never allowing him any favor ; and he was quite content to wait so long as he could sing songs to her and overthrow other knights in her cause.   Hence he roamed all over the country, breaking lances with everybody, and composing wonderful songs and lays to his mistress.   To one of these songs he received a reply in a few lines, which, as he could not read and his secretary was not with him, he was obliged to keep unread for ten days till the arrival of that important functionary, who read him eight lines of rhymes wherein the princess simply remarked, that " it is foolish to wish for what you must not have," and that " many a one speaks what his heart has no knowledge of." This was but cold comfort to Ulrich.

At the great festival which Leopold of Austria gave in 1225 to celebrate the reconciliation between two of his princes, Ulrich surpassed himself, and sent a messenger with a new song to his lady to tell of his mighty deeds. She had heard already of his achievements and admired the song, but suggested that his glory had been altogether overrated. Poor Ulrich became terribly downcast, sang a song of dreary winter, and when the next summer came went again in quest of tourneys, breaking innumerable lances in honor of his lady-love; on one of which occasions one of his fingers was nearly cut off. His messenger having been sent to the princess with a new song, brought back as her first expression of sympathy her regret that he had suffered a wound in her service, and at the same time a song written in a metre then unknown in Germany (an Italian song), which the princess requested Ulrich to translate into German. This he did at once, and dispatched his production back, receiving by the returning messenger a little dog as a token of her appreciation — such a dog as Tristan received from Isolde. Ulrich had never seen so beautiful a dog. With his wounded finger he returned to his mistress's country, and finding a faithful servant on the way, dispatched him with a new song to the princess, and instructed him to intercede with her that she might grant him the

meed of love after so many years of faithful service.
The lady listened approvingly to the song, but as for
love would not hear of it. Even a king might not
aspire to her favor.

Then Ulrich resolved to meet her resistance by in-
cessant endeavor. He went to Rome, stayed there
two months, and then returning, sent his mistress two
new songs, at the receipt of which she upbraided the
messenger for his boldness in pestering her still with
his master's love when she wanted none of it, particularly as she had recently heard that Ulrich had by
no means lost a finger in her service, as the messenger had reported to her. The messenger explained
that the finger had been healed, though so as to be
almost useless now. "I don't grudge him his finger,"
was the reply; "but I won't believe his messenger
any more since he has told me a lie." When Ulrich
heard this reproof he at once resolved to remove the
bone, or rather the finger of contention ; and one of
his friends, by his orders, struck it off at a blow with
a sharp knife. He then composed a most artistic
poem, and had a green-velvet case made with two
golden covers, and clasps in the shape of two small
hands, and in it he deposited the poem and the finger. Ulrich felt as glad as a school-boy who has succeeded in some ingenious trick that he had by this
stratagem forced his lady to think of him again ; and
sure enough she received the poem and finger with
expressions of sympathy mingled with feminine joy
at such devotion, concluding her remarks with the
sage observation that she had never believed a sensi-
ble man would do such a thing. She intended, she

sent him word, to keep the finger and look at it every day. This, however, she added, would not help the cause of his love.

Ulrich was so delighted with this message — which, like all messages from his lady-love, he received kneeling — that he resolved to undertake, in the service of his mistress, one of the maddest adventures ever conceived. He asked her permission, which was granted, and then at once made his preparations. Giving out that he was going on a pilgrimage to Rome, he arrayed himself in the garb of a pilgrim, left his castle Lichtenstein, and wandered on foot out of the country. When he came to Venice he stopped at a small tavern, and ordered to be secretly prepared for him twelve white ladies' dresses, thirty fine chemise-sleeves, three white velvet cloaks, and two ladies' head-dresses adorned with pearls. He then engaged twelve foreign servants who did not know his name, dressed them all in white clothes, bought white helms, shields, and a hundred white spears for himself and his followers, and white saddles, bridles, and dressings for his horses ; and thus prepared, sent thirty days before his own departure a messenger with an open letter to all the knights of Lombardy, Austria, Bohemia, etc., telling them that on the 24th of April the Goddess of Love, Venus, would arise from the Venetian sea and travel northward to Bohemia ; that every knight who met her and broke a lance with her should receive from her a golden ring having the power to beautify his lady-love and keep her true to him ; that every knight who might be dismounted by the lance of Venus must engage himself to bow to all the four quarters of the world in honor of a lady, but that the knight who succeeded in dismounting her should receive all her horses. Furthermore, he said that her face and her hands would be covered on the way, and that she would speak with no one ; that on the eighth day after the end of her travels she would open a tournament at Neuburg ; and that each knight who heard of this expedition of Venus and did not meet her, should be solemnly put under the ban of all true ladies.

On the appointed day, April 24th, Ulrich von Lichtenstein started on this Quixotic expedition. He rode on horseback, dressed in his gorgeous female attire of velvet and satin ; white silk gloves covered his hands, white sleeves his arms, and a thick white veil his face, while a magnificent coiffure towered on his head, from which two long pearl-embroidered braids hung down to his waist : surely the strangest impersonation of Venus ever conceived by the most chivalric brain of those chivalric times. He was preceded by his twelve squires, all dressed in white and carrying a white banner ; two white-dressed maids, and a half-dozen or so of fiddlers, trumpeters, and flute-players. An immense multitude assembled to witness his departure, and crowds greeted him at every station where he stopped. At one station two hundred women gathered to accompany him to mass, shouting loud : " Long live Queen Venus ! " In this way he got many kisses ; for his sex, though well known, was disregarded by the ladies, who chose to treat the close-veiled knight in his woman's dress as one of their own. Passing thus from place to place, he fought an untold number of knights. In Vienna, where his journey ceased and where he resumed his knightly clothes, it was calculated that he had broken three hundred and seven lances, distributed two hundred and seventy-one rings, and dismounted four knights. In no encounter had he himself ever been shaken in his saddle. Knights and princes proclaimed this achievement as one without a peer, the fame of which would last throughout all ages.

Soon after his return Ulrich met his faithful messenger, who brought him the woeful news that his mistress, the princess, would have nothing more to do with him, having heard that he now served another lady. This message threw Ulrich into a dreadful plight. He wept and moaned, wrung his hands, and raved like a madman. His friends tried to console him, but without avail. The blood burst out of his mouth and nose in a violent paroxysm of his agony, and it was not till his messenger promised to try his luck with the cold-blooded princess once more that Ulrich at all recovered his usual temper. During the absence of that faithful squire, Ulrich went home to his " dearest spouse, who could not be dearer to me than she is, although I have chosen another woman for my lady." For this erotic knight had a wife ; a wife, moreover, who seems to have been a very estimable woman, and had borne him several children ; nay, his "lady," the princess, was also a married woman.

This time the messenger had better luck. The lady received him graciously, listened attentively to the song sent by Ulrich, and seemed altogether on

the point of yielding. She had heard of Ulrich's behavior in Vienna, his weeping, mourning, and hemor-
rhage, which latter circumstanceseemed above all to
have melted her womanly heart. So she appointed
an interview, but stated expressly that she did not in-
tend to grant him any favor, and moreover stipulated
that he should come dressed as a leper, and in company with the other lepers to whom on Sunday morn-
ings she used to distribute alms. This was certainly
not only a cruel but also on the part of a lady a
rather unbecoming stipulation. Ulrich, however, was
but too glad to receive such a gracious communica-
tion, and rode some hundred and fifty miles in twenty
hours, killing two horses, to keep the appointment at
the proper hour. He put on leper's clothes, and
joining the disgusting crowd, approached the lady's
castle. One of the princess's maids served them
with food, and whispered to Ulrich that her lady
could not see him that day, and, indeed, not before
next evening. Ulrich, rather than stay with the lepers
over night, went into a corn-field, where he passed a
wretched night amidst rain, storm, and cold. When
the morn came he warmed himself by running, but
was still all wet when he appeared at the castle gates.
The maid sympathized with his great troubles, but
told him to defer his hopes till the night. Never in
his life did he pass so long a day ; and when night
came he hid himself in a ditch until a light appeared
at his lady's window. Then he crept stealthily to the
spot, where a rope was thrown down to draw him up.
But mark the Quixotic sequel. So long as his squire
could push Ulrich, who was clinging to the rope, all

went well ; but scarcely had Ulrich got beyond his squire's utmost reach when the fair hands who drew the rope in the lady's chamber gave way, and down he dropped — he with most rueful countenance. Three times did the experiment terminate thus unsuccessfully. Then Ulrich bethought him that his squire was not of so heavy a frame as himself, and by great effort the squire was successfully raised to the lady's room ; where, being mistaken by the lady for Ulrich himself, he was received with a loving kiss, "whereat she often afterwards felt ashamed." With the squire's assistance Ulrich was finally pulled up, and entered the sanctuary of his many years' hopes.

The lady lay abed, finely dressed, and surrounded by eight waiting-maids — very lovely but very superfluous, the noble knight thought. Nor could the hundred lamps that shone from the walls, the two great chandeliers at the bottom of the bed, the beautiful canopy of the bedstead, and the exquisite velvet mattress covered by two silk coverlets, which formed the other chief ornaments of the room, atone for the presence of these lovely attendants. But Ulrich's fervent prayers to have them dismissed were of no avail. The lady counseled the Knight of Lichtenstein to dismiss from his mind all thoughts of love, and stated that it was only on account of his recent extraordinary expedition in her honor that she had admitted him to her chamber, an honor never before granted to another man than her husband. As Ulrich declared that happen what might he would not leave his lady's presence until the morning, she finally had recourse to stratagem. She asked him to go

down the rope again, keeping hold of her hand for
surety, and let her pull him up once more. This he
did ; and when he was lowered a little way, she asked
him to lift up his head to kiss her, swearing she had
never loved man like him. Poor Ulrich let go her
hand to kiss her lips, and — down he tumbled in such
a terrific manner that it was a miracle he did not die.
Maddened with pain and anger he hurried off to a
river close by, resolved to drown himself. But his
squire caught him in time, and implored him to desist
from so mad an act. Finally, by dint of repeating
new promises, which the squire represented as coming from the cruel princess, this faithful servant got
Ulrich to take courage again. The lady, as the
squire alleged, had excused herself by saying that the
sudden entrance of an unfaithful maid had compelled
her to so cruel a proceeding, and that she had
pledged herself soon to admit him to her favor.
Meanwhile, Ulrich was to return to his castle and
wife ; which the rueful knight did.

Having thus quieted his master, the messenger
reported all the circumstances to the princess, who
seemed pleased enough with the knight's devotion,
but in another freak of coquetry sent him word that
he must join the next Crusade in her service. Ulrich
was delighted to be able to do something for his
mistress's glory, and sent her a glowing poem descrip-
tive of her unparalleled kindness and his unparalleled
bliss and glory in that his noble lady had permitted
him to go and fight for God and the cross in her
service. For this poem and a new song she returned
him her kindest thanks, and bid him prepare himself

for the Holy Land, but not to leave till he had been called by her to another meeting. Ulrich, who was enjoying himself in Vienna with other ladies, fighting and singing for them in true knightly fashion, when he received this message, fell into an ecstasy of joy, and sang some more songs in honor of the princess ; the great beauty of which songs so melted the heart of the woman that she relieved him from the Crusade, and bade him stay with her. In the full enjoyment of her love Ulrich passed two years of roaming, singing, and tourneying — two very happy years, as he says, during which his songs were being made known all over the country, both knights and ladies admiring their charming melodies and elegant composition. About the end of that time, however, his lady, the princess, played him a trick of so outrageous a nature that Ulrich dares not tell what it was. Probably she took some other lover. So, in the way of all offended lovers down to this day, Ulrich took to abusing the whole sex, and wrote some very bitter songs which were greatly admired, not only by the men but also and perhaps more by the ladies, who of course knew what was the occasion of those songs, Ulrich's love of the princess having become a matter of common talk — and who liked nothing so well than to have one of their own sex abused. Ulrich's princess, however, from whom he had formally separated, quitting her service, was enraged at these terrific sarcasms, and through some female friend Ulrich was finally persuaded to leave off singing satirical songs.

Now a lover who has been discarded, after he has

exhausted his vituperation of the sex in general, usually endeavors to fall in love with some other one of the sex in particular; and Ulrich, though a married man and of respectable years, thought it incumbent upon himself to act as a true knight of the period. He reflected, namely, that no true knight should be without a lady-love in whose service he might perform his wonderful deeds; and having made this reflection, he chose from the ladies of Germany the one above all most womanly, beautiful, good, chaste, gentle, and lovely. Having chosen, Ulrich was naturally in great hurry to tell the chaste one of his selection and adoration, which she accepted without much resistance, and thereby made Ulrich the happiest of men. Ulrich sang for her the most passionate songs his genius could contrive. But neither songs nor tourneys were a sufficient reward for the love of this paragon of all women: it was absolutely necessary, Ulrich thought, that he should undertake an enterprise for his new love as glorious at least as the one he had undertaken for the princess. Accordingly the noble knight, now some thirty-six years of age, dressed himself up in gorgeous style as King Arthur. He issued a proclamation that he had come from his fabled resting-place near the St. Graal to restore the order of the Round Table. The line of his travels was laid down and all knights challenged to meet him. Those who succeeded in breaking three lances with the King were to be rewarded by receiving the honor of wearing one of the names of the knights of the Round Table. A grand tourney was to end the expedition.

The excitement this proclamation produced was tremendous. People gathered from all quarters to witness the passing of King Arthur, who for some time encountered no knight strong enough to break three lances with him, but finally succeeded in surrounding himself with a Gawain, Lancelot, Tristan, Parcival, etc. These now followed all his movements, and considered this achievement the most glorious of all deeds they had ever done. Even Prince Frederic of Austria congratulated Ulrich upon the glory and success of his adventure, and it was only on account of political disturbances that the final tourney had to be postponed. The lady was, of course, vastly delighted with the glory Ulrich's adventure cast upon her, and with the beautiful songs he dispatched to her during his journey.

Some time after this achievement a sore calamity befell the knight; an event characteristic enough of the degeneracy which was then already beginning to set upon an era of high grandeur and brilliancy. Two knights, followers and friends of Ulrich, turned traitors and took him prisoner. Having first enticed all his servants and men from the castle, they surprised him with some of their own fellows, captured him and kept him in confinement. His wife they drove away from the castle, telling her that her husband would not be set free until he had given up to them all his possessions. His sons they kept in the castle as additional hostages. Ulrich's wife spread the news of the disaster over the neighborhood, and soon got together some three hundred of Ulrich's friends to rescue him. But Ulrich's jailers took their prisoner to a window with a rope around his neck, and told the outside multitude that on the first sign of an attack upon the castle Ulrich should be hung. Ulrich himself advised his friends to depart. He was thus held a captive for a whole year, and cruelly treated all the time, being often threatened with death by his tormentors, who tried to make him assign to them all his possessions. Yet his spirit remained undaunted, so that even during his captivity he was able to compose a new song for his lady-love. His liberation finally took place through the Duke of Görz coming to his assistance with some of his soldiers. Yet Görz was also forced to conclude a compromise with the two traitor knights ; and although we do not know what sum Ulrich had to pay for his ransom, it seems to have been a very heavy one.

But once more free, Ulrich soon forgot all the discomforts and costs of his confinement, in the enjoyment of his lady's love, which filled his heart with gladness. He kept up this sort of life till his death, which occurred about 1274–1277 ; so that he reached the age of seventy-five years. Nothing is known of his later life beyond that in 1268 he was arrested — conveniently it seems, and for purposes of extortion — on a charge of rebellion against King Ottocar, and kept imprisoned for about half a year, when he purchased his ransom with his two castles Lichtenstein and Muvan. He retained the castle Trauenburg, where he probably died. He has left, besides other songs, two large poems, the first one, "Frauendienst" (Woman's Service), composed by him in 1256, and the other one, " Frauenbuch " (Woman's Book), composed in 1259, when he had been a knight in woman's service for thirty-five years, and was about fifty-nine years old. The first poem is the one from which this sketch of his life is taken. It is a narrative poem of some fifteen thousand couplets, interspersed with the songs he sang to his ladies ; the " Frauenbuch " is a smaller narrative poem. It was absolutely fit that this Quixotic knight — of noble descent, possessed of vast estates and wealth, the father of a family, and husband of an estimable lady, whom he also loved, and who yet passed his life chiefly in roaming over the country in the service of other ladies, fighting and singing for them — should before the close of his career sit down to tell in minute detail all these follies of his life with a self-complacency and serious admiration of his great achievements that are really delightful. He has no more notion of having been a fool than of having been a faithless husband ; he considers himself a model knight, who has duly spent his life and strength in the service of the ladies. The sober way in which he tells his princess that in enjoying her love he will be drawn all the nearer to heaven and finish the accomplishments of a true Christian knight, is often astounding. This simplicity, which characterizes the whole large poem of his autobiography, does much to reconcile one with Ulrich. Besides, he is a genuine poet and artist. Though loving fighting above all things, to such an extent that he could not even find time to learn to read and write, he had studied the art of minstrelsy thoroughly.

For poetical composition was at that time held as a true art, requiring hard study and great experience, such a study of rhythm, language, and music as even the most thorough poets of modern times do not undertake. And Ulrich's songs are particularly distinguished by almost perfect purity of rhyme and great elegance of rhythmical construction. Indeed, they seem to have become very popular already in Ulrich's time, and were sung all over the country.

One of his most admired songs is the following : —

> — Lovely woman, sainted woman,
>   Woman thou most blest and good,
> — Ah, I fear thou'st felt for no man
>   Love's sweet passion in thy blood.
> — For if love to thee were known,
>   Thy small red mouth would have shown
>   Signs of sighs, thou blessèd one !
>
> — " Ah, but tell me, sir, what *is* love ?
>   Is't a woman or a man ?
> — I have ne'er yet learned of this love,
>   How it comes and goes again.
> — This, sir, you must let me know :
>   How it is, was, and doth grow ;
>   I may then guard 'gainst its woe."
>
> — Lady, love has such resources :
>   Every land doth it obey ;
> — And so manifold its forces —
>   I will tell you what I may :
> — Love is evil, love is good,

Weal and woe flow in its flood!
Lo, thus stands it with love's mood.

Tell me, sir, can love e'er lighten
  Sorrow and this life's distress?
High resolves within us brighten,
  Cherish good and worthiness?
Surely if love has that hold
On our lives as you have told,
Its bliss must be manifold."

— Lady, I will say, moreover:
  Love's reward brings wondrous bliss;
— It to rapture leads the lover,
  Leads him to all worthiness.
— Eye's enjoyment, heart's sweet play
Giveth love to all who may
With its blessings favored stay.

— "Tell me, sir, what gains a maiden
  Who love's guerdon haps to win?
— Is that heart with sorrow laden,
  Wheresoe'er love enters in?
— I'm too weak much grief to bear:
Shall I gain but grame and fear?
This is what I long to hear."

— Lady, grant my suit now slighted,
  And the mystery will be known;
Let our beings be united
  Till we both are only one.
As thou mine so I am thine. —

"Sir, this offer I decline ;
Be you yours and I stay mine."

The following three songs are in Ulrich's most musical vein, and seem, even in their English dress, proof
of his high rank as a Minnesinger. Indeed, so far as
grace and exquisite finish is concerned, Ulrich von
Lichtenstein's poems are the best of all Minnelieder,
nor does he ever in them descend to the coarseness
of Nithart or Tanhuser. German literary critics
seem to have underrated his poetical ability from
sheer scorn at the folly of his life : —

LOVE SONG.

— Ah, why care we for the morrow ?
        Joy is good.
— From the women we must borrow
        Lightsome mood.
— Happy who can win its blessing,
    Faith, he is a happy man :
Joy we gain from love's caressing,
    Honor follows e'er its van.

— We must, dancing, laughing, singing,
        Ever learn
— From fair women ; to them clinging
        Man can earn
— Worthily their love and favor,
    If he serves them faithfully.
Who repents their service ever
    With great grief will covered be.

— Fire by water is extinguished
    With much ease :
— Sunshine by the dark is vanquished ;
    True are these
— Stories both ; but hearken to one
    Who has felt it in his heart :
From heart's grief a true man no one
    But a woman e'er can part.

— Alas me, love ! I am flowing
    O'er with woe :
— Touch me, feel my pulses glowing !
    Coldest snow
—Would be quickly set a-burning
    By my heart's consuming heat.
Love, if thou canst help my yearning,
    Turn to me with pity sweet !

TO THE BELOVED.

Blessèd the feeling
That taught me the lesson thou hearest
    — Gently appealing :
To love thee the longer the dearest,
    — And hold thee nearest ;
    Yea, as a wonder
    From yonder, that bearest
    Rapture the wildest,
Thou mildest, thou purest, thou clearest.

    —-I faint, I die, love,
With ecstasy sweetest and rarest,

— When thou draw'st nigh, love,
And me thy sweet pity declarest.
— Then, as thou sharest
Love, O, I'll sing thee
And bring thee bonairest
Redress, and over
Thee hover, thou sweetest, thou fairest.

— My hands I fold, love,
And stay at thy feet, humbly kneeling,
— Till, like Isolde, love,
Thou yield to the passionate feeling
— O'er thy heart stealing;
Till thy behavior's
Sweet favors reach healing
My heart, and tender
Love's splendor to thee be revealing.

— I pray but send me
A hope, ere my locks shall turn gray, love,
— Thou wilt befriend me,
And I of thy grace catch a ray, love.
— To light my way, love
Thine eyes were fated
And mated: their sway, love,
My soul beguiling
Shall smiling revive me for aye, love.

LOVE'S BLISS.

— Summer glow
Lieth low
Upon heath, field, wood, and grass.
— Here and there
In the glare,
White, red, gold peeps from the place.
— Full of joy
Laughs the sky,
Laughs what on the earth doth rove.
Happy man
He who can
Live so that all things him move
To love, to love.

— Whom God's grace
Gives no less
Than to live in love alway,
— May in faith
Ever bathe
In the sunny glow of May.
— He doth toy
With sweet joy
Whene'er called to be love's guest.
Sweet to live,
Love can give
To whome'er she loveth best.
Love is so blest.

— Whom a maid
E'er has had

Clasped in passionate embrace,
   — If he not
   Say'st, I wot,
Great his wrong is and disgrace.
   — But who true
   Telleth you
How sweet love him has addressed :
   Him each word
   Brings reward
When by tender arms he's pressed
   And caressed.

   — Treasured hoard
   Is each word
Which in kisses overflows ;
   — When they gay
   Play love's play,
Loving limb to limb clings close.
   — With eyes bright
   From love's light
They each other look upon.
   Ah, forsooth,
   Then, in truth,
Such a love by each is shown :
   Greater none.

   — Lover's bliss
   Fully is
Realized whene'er a man
   — And a maid
   Thus are laid
In love's fond embrace, and when

    — Kiss on kiss
    Highest bliss
Into both pours with love's spell.
    Whether not
    More be sought?
Ah, the small red mouth doth tell
    By its swell —
    But soon grows well.

The following, if it is really by Lichtenstein, was probably written in the later period of his life : —

  — Where have joy and honor vanished?
Where are all good teachings banished?
World, thy manners are ill-planished,
    Thy praise limpeth on a staff.
  — Courteous shone thy crown forever
What time men won woman's favor
Without guile, in chaste endeavor ;
    Thou hast cast it off as chaff.
  — Of pure woman hearty greeting
Would set often grief retreating
From the head to feet, and beating
    Anxious hearts cause 'gain to laugh.

  — Woman, thy name joy enhances ;
God on thee showers blissful trances ;
Thy life knows no dissonances,
Of sure comfort thou'rt a roof.
  — Woman all unwomanliness flying,
Ne'er let shame on thee be prying ;

That thy glory stay undying
    Keep thou from all taint aloof.
— For if falseness be thy lover,
O'er thy name disgrace will hover;
Yea, thy name with scandal cover,
    And a checkmate to thee proof.

— Knighthood, how stands now thy order?
Where is now thy worth's recorder?
We saw thee erst virtue's hoarder;
Ah, how proud flashed then thy glance!
— Now the women mourn, the lusty,
That thy shield stays cobwebbed, dusty,
Wholly unused and untrusty.
    Where thy tourney now, and dance?
— Thy life thou so keep'st betraying:
Even shame abhors thy staying,
Her powers on the street displaying, —
    Once more take up honor's lance!

CHAPTER VI.

THE METRICAL ROMANCES OF THE MINNESINGER,
AND GOTTFRIED VON STRASSBURG'S "TRISTAN
AND ISOLDE."

PART from the knightly and even from the citizen Minnesinger, stood the bards of the people, who chanted the hero-deeds of the nation, the ballads of the Nibelungen and of Kudrun. They also employed, as the singing requires, the strophe-form, but their strophes had not the triplicity of form which distinguish the Minnesong. Unknown, unremembered, these bards have passed away, leaving but those two weird epics for posterity to admire in wonder and fit them, as best one may, to the graciousness of the Minnesong, with which they were contemporary.

But there was another class of epic poems produced in that period, which blends more readily with the Minnepoetry, and indeed was fostered by the same men who sang the Minnelieder. This class comprises a vast number of metrical romances or narrative poems, most of which were occasioned by, and partly translated from the Provençal poets, and had for their subjects the legends of King Arthur's Round Table and of Charlemagne's Peers. Gottfried of Monmouth's Chronicles, and the Crusades, had spread the legend gathered around those two great heroes over all Europe and Asia, where they became strangely commingled with innumerable local traditions and historical data.

To this commingling process the addition of the two most prominent personages in those legends is to be ascribed: Tristan, the lover of Isolde, and Parcival, the heir to the crown of the mystic St. Graal. But not all of these metrical romances have these legends for their subjects; one of the finest of them, the "Poor Henry" of Hartmann von der Aue, is the original of that sweet story of self-sacrifice, which Longfellow has made universally known as the "Golden Legend."

Some of these romances are written in strophes; but by far the greater number in a very peculiar form of metre, which for want of a better name may be called here the narrative metre, and the fundamental rule of construction whereof is, that it proceeds in rhymed couplets, each line of which has, if the rhyme is masculine, *four*, and, if the rhyme is feminine, *three* accentuations; and each line of which must nave not less than five nor more than ten syllables. This rule was first formally fixed by Heinrich von Veldeke, the father of Minnepoetry. Coleridge, in his poem of "Christabel," has in part adopted this metre, though, as usual with him, without acknowledging its source.

An old English piece of poetry, that has the same metre, is mentioned by Walter Scott, "Tristram," Introd. cxix.

Now that lines of a given number of accentuations

or feet — in music we say beats — should have op-
tionally five or ten syllables, seems barbarous rude-
ness to those who look upon rhythm as anything else
than the mere relation of sounding time-moments to
each other. To a musician it is as clear as sunlight,
that four beats of common or triplet music may have
any number of notes, provided the instruments can
play them fast or slow enough to keep the time ; why
then should not a poet within his four beats or feet of
rhythm gather as many or few syllables as he chooses,
provided the tongue can utter them sufficiently quick
or slow to fill the accentuations ? If the musician
can rest his rhythm with exquisite effect on long
notes or syncopations, as Beethoven loves to do, why
should not the poet be allowed to check his rhythm
all at once, and rest slowly upon monosyllabic feet, if
he can but find the proper long syllables ? If the
musician can alternate $\frac{3}{4}$ and $\frac{2}{4}$ time, as modern music
loves to do within a few beats, why may not the
poet modulate suddenly from trochaics to anapæsts?
That such a free rhythmical construction will not
answer for songs is evident enough ; songs have a
fixed melody, that, once established, must remain
precisely the same for all strophes ; but for the narrative, the raconteur-style, this constantly varying,
and yet in the main, in the accentuation, uniform
rhythm seems to me most admirably adopted. It requires, however, a skillful reader, and from those un-
accustomed to it, ready attention.

Amongst the number of metrical romances that
are left to us of that time, three tower above all the
rest: Hartmann von der Aue's " Golden Legend of

Poor Henry," in which that sweet story is told in the sweetest, simplest manner, within a compass of some fifteen hundred lines ; Wolfram von Eschenbach's " Parcival ;" and, most excellent of all, Gottfried von Strassburg's " Tristan and Isolde."

It may be interesting to stop for a moment to a comparison of the way in which the same subjects have been treated by those poets and the foremost of our own age ; and now that Tennyson's " Idylls" have been completed, such a judgment as to the merits of his work in comparison with the works of these Minnesinger is surely not improperly made. The judgment of such literary works of art decides, of course, in regard to the two chief points : —

1. With respect to the development of the plan of the work which forms its subject, as to whether the sentiments and actions portrayed follow each other in the best possible sequence, gathering around a common central point ; and if an historical plan has been chosen, whether all the points furnished by it have been used to the greatest advantage ; as also whether, in the description of the characters sketched, attention has been paid to historical, and, above all, to psychological truth.

2. With respect to the execution of the plan, whether the most suitable metre or metres, or perhaps also strophe-forms have been chosen ; whether the vast resources of rhyme and rhythm have been abundantly and skillfully made use of ; whether similes have been used judiciously, and words chosen with proper art ; and whether these various forms and appliances of art have been so masterly turned

to use with practiced hand, that no trace of labor and effort is left to tell tales.

This second point we need not here consider, beyond expressing an opinion that blank verse rhythm and measure seems especially limited to dramatic uses, and becomes feeble in a corresponding ratio as it is employed for narrative purposes. In Shakespeare it has its element; in Milton it develops wondrous strength, as the dramatic effects ripen; in the "Idylls" it does many splendid things, but more generally falls into insipidity. Swinburne, in his "Prelude to Tristan and Isolde," has shown the right art-spirit in the selection of his metre; and even more than usually a wonderful mastery of rhythmic effects.

In regard to the first point, Tennyson in taking up an historical subject, has certainly remained true to almost the only feature of that subject which seems properly to claim historical truth; that is, the infidelity of Queen Guinevere; but in doing so, has sacrificed the predominant interest of art. In arranging the adventures which legendary lore of that subject furnished him, around this historical point, King Arthur, the chief figure of his story, not only lost the dignity and nobleness of character which art absolutely demanded, but became even a positive object of contempt. For the representation in art of a cuckold is always more or less disgusting, from the simple fact that he necessarily excites our contempt in that he is overcome by a superior in a point wherein, above all others, he ought to have made valid his claim to our sympathy: in his love. If *she* cannot

13

acknowledge his superiority, we certainly cannot. There was no necessity that Tennyson should have made this artistic blunder. He could have treated the same legends, and remained quite as true to their historical truth, had he gathered those tales around the figure of one of the noblest of the Round Table Knights, throwing King Arthur and Guinevere's shame as much as possible into the background. This was all the more the proper way, in that those legends had in themselves a great central drama of surpassing artistic beauty and interest in the St. Graal mystery ; and this was the course adopted by Wolfram von Eschenbach in his treatment of the same legends.

This Wolfram von Eschenbach, — so named from his birthplace, Eschenbach, a village near Nuremberg, — a knight of noble birth, had, like Walther, being a second son, been driven by poverty to earn his living by knightly services or tuneful minstrelsy. Like all his fellow knights and minstrels, he was a homeless wanderer ; yet most of his time seems to have been spent in the service of the generous and art-loving Prince Hermann of Thüringen. Eschenbach died about the year 1228, fully appreciated by his age, as he indeed was appreciated for nearly three centuries afterwards ; his great poem, " Parcival," having been one of the first books printed after the invention of printing. The date of that first publication of " Parcival" is 1477. His other preserved larger work is entitled " Titurel," although it deals only with an episode of the history of that famous King of the Graal: the love-episode of " Sigure and Schionatulander." Eschenbach did not finish it. The fragment preserved to us has only some one hundred and seventy strophes, of seven lines each, in the Minnelieder fashion ; yet these one hundred and seventy strophes are held by all competent critics to constitute one of the finest productions of German lyrical poetry, and a crowning glory of Eschenbach's age.

But to return to Parcival. Eschenbach, seizing upon the central point of the King Arthur legends with the eye of a true artist, took for his main subject the solemn mystery of the St. Graal, and around it gathered in glowing description the variety of incidents furnished by those legends. The religious earnestness which prompted the design, is plainly enough indicated by the titles of the three books, into which the poem is divided : Simplicity, Doubt, Salvation. The mastery with which the multitude of adventures of the twenty-five thousand lines of this are arranged to serve the main purpose of the story ; the glorious picture of the meditative child Parcival, growing up in this strange world of knighthood ; the magnificent contrast of the figure of the Red Knight, Parcival, as, turned out from the Temple of the Graal, he storms in vain search and despair through the world, looming up every now and then amidst King Arthur's revels and fights ; and the final reconciliation of the worn-out soul with God and the St. Graal, — all these are matters that have been the admiration of men from Eschenbach's to the present time. Tennyson had the same subjects to choose, but instead of Sir Parcival, selected the utterly inane figure of Galahad.

Or, if Tennyson was determined to make the

other distinctive feature of these legends, the love-passion, the chief theme of his work, rather than the religious element of the St. Graal, he had at hand in one of his legends that very same relation between the sexes which existed between Queen Guinevere and Launcelot, and yet deprived in the essential point of all disgusting characteristics.   It seems strange that the impropriety of making this adulterous connection between the king and queen the chief theme of his song should not have struck Tennyson, when he dedicated his legends to the husband of Queen Victoria, even in that dedication drawing comparisons; strange that he should have taken no means to hide it, by at least bringing the king into some position of interest, where his actions would proclaim his fitness to enchain our interest in some degree; whereas he is made so little of, that he seems a mild, inoffensive, gentle soul, who is ready even to shake hands with the seducer of his wife. With what consummate art does Gottfried von Strassburg seize every opportunity to devise some means to bring forth King Mark into interesting and noble positions; so that *his* cuckoldom may not lower him too much in our eyes.   Nor is Mark ever made to connive at his own disgrace in Gottfried's version of the legend of "Tristan and Isolde;" that legend, which Tennyson might have chosen — discarding Parcival and the St. Graal — as the central point of his work; a legend, which even now again stirs up the world as it stirred up the Middle Ages beyond all others of its kind.

That which gives this legend this rare charm and

power is the fact that its subject is the highest power of that wonderful feeling which from the first days of the world's existence has been recognized and celebrated as love, and the veriest glory of which lies in self-sacrifice of one for another, and the thus making a veritable one of twain. In defiance of all sneers and persecutions, in spite of all its own errors, this feeling lives as it has lived, and will forever continue to live, the almighty ruler of the world. In this, its almightiness, lies both its wonderful bliss and the source of its tragical elements wherever it comes into collision with the opposing forces which the life on earth raises against it. Having its source in itself, utterly absolute in this its essence and origin, it admits of no why or wherefore of its ground. It exists between these two beings, between this man and this woman, *because* it exists, and so existing without a ground endureth necessarily forever and ever. Its very absolute character, which to the superficial glance makes it seem fitful and subject to all possibilities of change, holds it immutable in the region where change never enters. Tennyson's lines, —

> " And therefore is my love so large for thee,
> Seeing it is not bounded save by love,"

suggest the ground of love's immutability and omnipotence with perfect accuracy, and — however paradoxical it may seem — on that very account the perishability and impotence he seemingly intends alone to convey. Conscious of this its immutable and all powerful character, love endureth all things and overcometh all things; but in this effort to endure and overcome meets all those earthly resistances that, as already said, give rise to its tragical catastrophes, — the catastrophes that make up seven eighths of our dramas and novels or poems; and the fact that earthly life can oppose no severer obstacles to the strength and might of love than the mournful history of Tristan and Isolde presents, is the very one that has given to this legend its universal popularity and preëminent qualification for poetical treatment.

Indeed, the merely enduring power of love affords but little scope for artistic representation to excite interest, the element of beauty being overbalanced by the element of ugliness which calls for the endurance. The comedian may use it in art, but even he has to handle his representation carefully. The endurance of love shines forth chiefly after marriage, and consists in a miraculous sacrifice of all selfish interests, down to the pettiest details of habit, life, and longing. To him who sees it exhibited, and to whom at the same time the ground of the endurance is visible, it is the most lovable, strengthening, comforting sight of life. To the careless glance it is ludicrous. By a strange perversity of human nature, love itself seems to share a glimpse of this ludicrous aspect of its glory; and so you will find the wife, from this perverted view, stir up the enduring husband, or the husband stir up the enduring wife by taunt, impertinence, disobedience, nay, downright rebellion, to a passion which shall break that endurance and cause both her or his own love to shine forth in its strength and overcoming almightiness, which otherwise would never have had a chance so to shine forth. In this perversity, heightened in woman by physical causes, lies the source of almost all the troubles of love-marriages.

It is, therefore, in the overcoming power of love — that is, where the power appears, for in endurance, though the power may be stronger, it is not manifested — that art revels; and as from the very nature of the case that power can be exercised in its highest intensity only against itself or a semblance of itself, so we find everywhere the highest collision of love to be a lover loving another's wife : Paris and Helen ; Sir Launcelot and Guinevere ; Tristan and Isolde. In this representation art must needs exhaust its supreme powers ; for not only is the highest glory and strength of love to be pictured, but the relation between the loved one and the husband whom she does not love, must be toned down to such a degree that it shall not excite disgust. It is in this that the preeminent art of Gottfried von Strassburg shows its supremacy. Compare with it not merely the contemporary versions of " Tristan and Isolde," but the very latest of Tennyson. In Tennyson's there is the fundamental defect of infidelity in both of the lovers, who in that legend's most numerous and beautiful versions are portrayed as unwaveringly faithful unto each other till death ; and the relation between Isolde and her lover receives from his pen an altogether unnecessary addition of the disgusting element, by the poet's making the excuse for her preference for Tristan over King Mark depend upon physical grounds ; and, as if this were not bad enough, the lovers them-

selves are represented as mocking at the ungainly
figure and long crane legs of the deceived husband.
Nothing but the irresistible power of the love-potion
can, even in Gottfried's delicate version, keep our
sympathy and pity for the unhappy faithless wife ; and
the merely amorous Isolde of Tennyson, who casts
her faith aside simply because Tristan's bodily per-
fections are greater than her husband's, not only
loses all our sympathy, but becomes an utterly unar-
tistic object of loathing and disgust when made herself to boast of this as her reason of preference ;
for even more contemptible than a cuckold, yea, the
most contemptible of all things is a lustful woman,
sacrificing the representation of her immortal and divine personality, the sacred majesty of her body, for
her own self's pleasure. In very proportion as that
sacrifice is the most exalted and glorious a woman
can make to a loved man, and which only woman has
the privilege and glory of being able to make, is it
unspeakably degrading to make it for herself ; no art
can afford to even breathe the name of a Messalina.

Gottfried von Strassburg, the greatest of all the
poets of the Minnesinger-period, wrote this poem,
which has some twenty thousand lines, in the years
1206–1215, following the manuscript of an old French
poet, whom he calls Thomas of Brittany, and who
was perhaps the first writer who gave literary shape
to this British story of all powerful and faithful love.
Of Gottfried's circumstances and life we know liter-
ally nothing, except that he was not a knight but a
citizen ; that he was a learned man, and that he enjoyed the esteem of all his contemporaries, except

that of Wolfram von Eschenbach, with whom he seems to have had a feud, he disliking Eschenbach's earnest, often very uncouth and strange speech, and Eschenbach equally disliking Gottfried's graciousness and worldly calm. So great was the esteem in which Gottfried's " Tristan " was held by his age, that two other poets attempted to finish his poem, he having left it unfinished, whilst many other Minnesinger in their poems lament the irreparable loss. Indeed, looking merely at the artist skill in the selection of a subject, how could a poet having for his object to sing the power of love have chosen a more judicious story than this, wherein that love's irresistible power need not be extolled by the subjective reflections of the poet, but manifests itself dramatically, in action, in constant efforts to elude a husband's claims and vigilance, in infamous deceit practiced by natures previously of rare nobility, and is even ready to commit crimes for the sake of its own satisfaction ? Or was any other subject so well adapted artistically to represent the absoluteness and blindness of love than this story, wherein that love appears as the result of a love potion ? For love has no rational ground in its sensuous aspect ; it is *because* it is, and refuses to account for itself ; but in representative art a sensuous ground is a necessity. Now, whereas painting can place this sensuous ground in beauty by painting it, a poet can never, through mere description of beauty, sufficiently inflame our fancy to make us consider the ground equal to the effect. We always forget the beauty of the woman, because it is not sensuously present, and are, therefore, ever impelled to ask

the lover, why do you act so foolishly ?   In the story
of Tristan and Isolde, however, this question is cut
off from the beginning ; they love because they cannot
help themselves ; they must, for they have drunken
the philter ; they have no freedom now, and are
powerless under the all-powerful influence of love.
By this means, the poet has also saved our sympathy
for the chief persons of his poem.   If they were
ordinary lovers, lustful, simply like Launcelot and
Guinevere, we should never overcome a feeling of
contempt for two persons committing crimes and
descending to the lowest deceit for the gratification
of their passion.   But the love potion takes away from
Tristan and Isolde all such ugliness.   Our sympathy
increases as we see the loyal, noble-hearted knight
giving slowly way and finally succumbing altogether :
and " Isolde la doux, Isolde la belle," even in a still
higher degree moves our pity, for in her natural con-
dition she hates in Tristan the murderer of her mother's brother.   With admirable taste and æsthetic
judgment has Gottfried von Strassburg represented
Tristan and Isolde as rather cold, or at least careless,
to each other during the long time that they are ac-
quainted before she goes on board the ship which
is to bring her to King Mark.   There is not a sign
of mutual attraction or unchaste desire until the un-
fortunate potion has been tasted.   This saves their
characters and our sympathy, and by a natural con-
sideration saves even our sympathy for King Mark.
In the true spirit of a classic drama, *fate* hurries these
three persons to destruction in a situation which
moves our intensest pity.

But to the excellence of his general arrangement of subject Gottfried adds a poetic beauty of diction, a wondrousness of melody of rhythm, sound of rhyme, mysterious alliteration, quaint reversions, and cunning refrain, the which no other of his contemporaries in this form of poetry even approaches. His refrain is of that most charming kind, which gives such rare beauty also to Goethe's second part of "Faust," and to Tennyson's "Maud;" a repetition in slightly varied form of certain passages, rhythms, rhymes, or similes, that have gone before unobserved, and never caused an expectancy of repetition.

Nor is Gottfried merely skillful. His poem abounds in the most charming thoughts, reflections, images, and pictures, and with the rare self-consciousness of a thorough master he handles every incident of his story.

That this is not too high praise, witness the following passages from that part of the poem where the fated lovers drink the love potion. In no story of first awakening love is the growth of this passion described with more exquisite beauty and psychological truth : —

TRISTAN AND ISOLDE DRINKING THE FATAL LOVE POTION.

— Meanwhile the ships their voyage made.
From the first day's start they had
Of wind and weather fairest spell ;
But now the women 'gan to fail.
Isolde and her women crew,
To whom the sea and wind were new,

And new the toil they had to bear:
It was not long until they were
Worn out with such unused distress.
To rest them from their weariness,
Tristan, the master, gave command
The ship should make for the nearest land.
Into a bay their course they drew;
Then went some of the crew
For jolly sports out on the land.
But Sir Tristan thought t'attend
On his charge, Isolde, and greet
By visit her as it was meet.
Now when he down by her sat —
Talking or of this or that,
Whatever came into their thought —
He asked that a drink to him be brought:
What time attending his dear queen
There was no one to be seen
But some small girls t'obey her sign.
One, beckoned thus, cried : " Here is wine !
At least I think it must be so."
Ah me, that fated flask did glow
With anything but wine, alas!
Although it looked so in the glass,
It held the growing heaviness,
The endless, weary heart-distress,
From which at last they both fell dead.
But neither knew this then; the maid
Went quick to where stood put away
The flask and drink — alack the day !
She offered it to Tristan first,
Who bade Isolde first quench her thirst.

She drank constrained and as if pained,
Then gave it him ; he quickly drained
The glass, and both thought they'd drank wine.
Just then Brangaene them did join ;
The flask she knew at once, and clear
The whole truth there flashed upon her ;
Whereat she felt such dreadful woe
That all her strength left her, as though
Her body were already dead.
With a dead heart then the maid
Arose and took the glass of woe,
And, staggering forward, cast it so
Into the wild and raging sea.
"Ah, woe is me ; ah, woe!" cried she,
"That birth was given me ever !
I, wretched one, shall never
Faith and honor regain for aye ;
May God repent and rue the day
That on this fatal trip I came !
That death kept me not from this shame,
When I t'accompany Isolde
Upon this dreadful ship, was told !
Ah, woe, Isolde ! and Tristan, woe !
That drink will prove your death I trow."

Now, when the virgin and the man
These two, Isolde and Tristan,
Had drank the drink : what chanced to them ?
Ah, then the world's unquiet came,
Love, the heart-huntress, and began
To slip in the hearts of maid and man

Before of it they were aware.
She raised her flag of victory there,
And without scarce a struggle drew
Into her power and glory the two.
They now grew one and all the same ;
Who had been two now one became :
They now no more could move apart.
Isolde's hatred had left her heart.
The mighty purifier, Love,
So wonderfully their soul gan move,
All hate from their hearts clearing,
And so with love them stirring,
That each one to the other was
Clear as the clearest mirror-glass.
They both together had but one heart,
His grief she took in equal part ;
Her pain oppressed him as his own.
They were both simply one
In sad and loving feeling,
Yet did they try concealing.
This was occasioned by doubt and shame ;
She felt ashamed and he the same.
She doubted him, he doubted her,
However blind their love might stir.
Flowing together in one glow,
Still lacked they courage in their woe
For the beginning and the first word ;
This kept confession long deferred.

Tristan, when love first stirred in him,
Began to think and reason grim
On honor and fidelity.

He wished to turn away and fly.
" No," thought he e'er and e'er again,
" No, Tristan, come and be a man,
And from this sin keep well aloof."
Yet suffered his heart no reproof.
Thus did he 'gainst his wish conspire,
Desired against his best desire.
It drew him off, it drew him on.
The entrapped, bewitched man, prone
To try, tried if by force perhaps
He could escape love's tightening grasps.
And long indeed held he out so.
The faithful one bore double woe:
One as the other his heart struck.
Whene'er into her eye he'd look,
Then by the power of mighty love
His heart and senses 'gan to move
And inmost soul to be consumed.
He thought of honor and faith entombed ;
But thus awhile gained victory then.
Immediately began again
His hereditary queen, sweet love,
To force him near her heart to move.
Faith and honor never
Gave up their endeavor ;
But love still did endeavor more,
And used him sorer e'en than sore ;
Worse than faith or honor either,
Nay, worse than both together.
Love looked sweet-smiling at his heart,
And cast into his eyen her dart.

But when love did not look at him,
His suffering was e'en still more grim.
Right often, too, he'd think, e'en as
Thoughts through a prisoner's mind will pass,
How he might banish all that pain.
He thus thought oft and oft again :
"Let me my heart elsewhere direct,
And change or alter its effect,
Love and pursue another light."
Then closed the sling and held him tight.
He oft his heart and senses took,
To seek some change in a secret nook,
But there was nothing in their hold,
Than love and his sweet queen Isolde.

Isolde in the same fashion
Tried the same with her wild passion.
In raging grief she flared, what time
She recognized the catching lime
Of that love alluring,
Which held and kept enduring
All her senses and her soul.
She tried to 'scape heart-free and whole,
And struggled to obtain release.
But ah ! the lime held her with ease,
And dragged her down despairing.
In vain she'd try proud bearing,
And struggle hard at every step ;
She struggled to get out of the trap,
And tried in vain at every end
With her foot and her hand.
She turned and twisted in every shape,

But more and more, ah sad mishap !
Sank her hands and feet again
In the blind sweetness of the man
And of his love's attraction.
Her soul from this lime's action
Could not again itself unloose,
Nor find a way or bridge, where close
Love did not follow everywhere,
At each half step that she took there.
Whate'er she pondered in her thought
Or to her mind, to dream of, brought,
It was no other subject than
Ever her love and her Tristan.
Now this she held concealed so far :
It was an everlasting war
Between the heart and 'tween the eye.
Shame caused her eye away to hie,
Whilst love in the heart found willing stay ;
And this fore'er conflicting sway
'Twixt maid and man, love and shame,
Made her confused as to her aim.
The maid hungered to have the man,
Yet turned her eye away again,
Whilst shame desired to love ; but so
That no one of its love might know.
What could this help her ? Shame and maid,
As all the world has often said,
Are so changing and fickle
That they can never mickle
Resistance to strong passion show.
Isolde let the war e'en go

14

As it might choose, and gave away ;
Vict'ryless ceding to the sway
Of the man and love combined
With her body and her mind.
Often his eye with hers she sought,
And secretly of him took note.
Her clear eyen and eke her heart
Now in peace acted their part.
Her heart and eyen went stealing,
Cautiously their way feeling,
And full of love, unto the man.
The man looked at her again
With tender and imploring mien ;
He too 'gan to yield within,
Since love would not relax its hold.
Thus Sir Tristan and Isolde
Gave each other every hour,
Whenever it was in their power,
Passionate eye-pleasure.
They each seemed each to treasure
More beautiful than e'er before ;
Love worked this wonder as of yore,
And still it works it, ruleth now,
And will forever rule, I trow.
Each year the lovers learn again
That they each other please more when
Love of them has taken hold ;
More flowers love's usury doth unfold,
And through its sweetness 'gin to grow,
Than in her first spring-time e'er blow.
Yea, usurious love still grows
After it first in th' heart arose ;

This is the seed which love doth sow,
Which nevermore may lay her low.

— Love seemeth sweeter than before,
Thus doth love's right its bloom restore ;
If love seemed ever as before,
No power could its lost bloom restore.

— The ships again from the coast had cleared,
And joyously their home-path steered.
Only two tender hearts therein
Mighty love now did begin
Far from their path to lead astray.
In deep thoughts sunk away
Both care and grief did borrow
From that dearest sorrow
Which, miracles fulfilling,
Honey to gall distilling,
Sweetness all sour can render ;
To fire the dew's wet splendor
And the gentle change to sadness,
Mild hearts turn to strange badness,
Which all the world doth turn awry ;
This sorrow 'twas which, to destroy
Tristan and the fair Isolde
Threatened with its grasping hold.
It weighed upon both equally.
Never rest upon the sea
Nor here nor there could find the twain
Till each the other saw again ;
And when they saw each other
Their looks they tried to smother,

Hindered by fear of duty
To revel in their beauty.
Strangeness it was, and eke a shame
Which ever their delight o'ercame.
If glance from glance sweet drinking,
Their eyes at last 'gan sinking
Into each other, when alone,
They ever colored and shone
Like to their mind and to their heart.
This was love's, the colorer's, art.
Love did not deem't enough to prey
On noble hearts in secret sway,
But longed to tell its story
And manifest its glory
By causing both at every hour
To testify of love's strange power.
Their color stayed not long the same,
Not long the same their color came.
It changed before you'd marked it well,
Pale with the red, the red with pale.
They now turned pale, they now turned red,
As love's emotions o'er them swayed.
Thereby in each did knowledge rise,
As could not well be otherwise,
That somewhat of love's burning,
Each to the other turning,
Must in all their senses move.
Then began they too with love
Upon each other much to dote,
And time and hour with care to note
When usually they together came.
Like true hunters of love's game,

With fondling looks they fastened
Their nets and traps ; and hastened
To fix nooses and gins for each.
They passed their time with cunning speech —
Questions and replies and play.
Isolde in her girlish way
Found for it the beginning.
Gently she neared him, winning
Quite from afar, as 'twere her way.
She asked : If he recalled the day
When he to Develin alone,
In a little boatlet thrown,
Sorely wounded and helpless had come ;
How her mother then him home
Had removed to cure his limb ?
This led her to say to him,
How herself, under his care,
Writing neatly had learned there ;
Latin too, and the harp to play.
Many such hints in his way,
Were by sweet Isolde thrown ;
And how his manliness had shown
In the fearful serpent-fight ;
How then she'd recognized the knight
In the wood and in the bath.
Their words pursued an equal path,
She'd speak to him and he reply.
" Alas ! " Isolde said, " that I
Neglected chance and checked just wrath,
And did not kill you in the bath.
O God ! what did possess me so ?
Had I known then what now I know,

Your death it had been verily."
" But why, my sweet Isolde ? " said he ;
"What worries you ; what is't you know ? "
" Yea, what I know, that is my woe,
What I see that worries me ;
The sky doth plague me, and the sea,
Life and body cause me fear."
With that she forward bent, and near,
With elbow against him 'gan to lean ;
Thus did their boldness first begin.
Her eyes, mirror-clear and holy,
Seemed to gather water slowly ;
Her heart began bounding,
Her sweet, small mouth rounding ;
Her head drooped on her shoulder.
Then again her friend to hold her,
With his arms drew nearer ;
Yet clasped he her not dearer,
Than to stranger she might have ceded.
Softly and sweetly he pleaded :
" O, sweet lady, let me know,
Why worry, why complain you so ? "
The shuttlecock of love, Isolde,
" Lameir," said she, " my woe I hold,
Lameir oppresses thus my heart ;
It is Lameir that makes me smart."
When she Lameir so often said,
Tristan then to reflect essayed,
And with anxious care to glean
What the little word might mean.
Then quick the remembrance came :
Ameir stood for love's sweet name,

Amer, for bitter, la mer for sea :
A herd of meanings there seemed to be.
He overlooked one of the three,
And but of two made inquiry ;
Love's sweet name concealing
The ruler of their feeling,
Their comfort, their desire and yoke ;
And but of sea and bitter spoke.
"I fear me," said he, "sweet Isolde,
That sea and fog have caused you cold,
That sea and wet winds cause you fear.
'Tis they, are bitter to you here."
"By no means, sir, why say ye so ?
Of both, faith, neither gives me woe,
Me worries neither sea nor air,
My only suffering is Lameir."

— When on that word's track thus he came,
As meaning love's sweet foreign name,
He whispered her quite secretly:
"Faith, sweet one, 'tis the same with me,
Lameir and you my woe I hold.
Sweet heart's ruler, dear Isolde,
You and your sweet love alone
Have my senses one by one
Sore confused and shaken.
From the straight path I'm taken
So forcibly, so far astray,
I never more shall find my way.
Me worrieth and annoyeth,
Me loatheth and destroyeth
Whatsoever meets my glance.
O, love, in all the world's expanse

My heart holds nothing dear but thee."
Isolde said : " Sir, so is't with me."

—When now the lovers 'suredly
Of one sense knew themselves to be
One single heart and eke one will,
Their grief it began to still ;
But also to betray their yoke.
Each of them both looked and spoke
Bolder to the other then ;
The man to the maid, the maid to the man.
That former strangeness left their whim :
He kissed her, she kissed him
With sweet and lingering kisses.
This was of their distresses
The first intoxicating draught.
Each one proffered then and quaffed
The sweetness which rose from the heart.
As often as they met apart
This love exchange 'tween them was made.
It almost seemed a smuggling trade,
For it went on so stealthily
That no one in the world did see
Their secret mind or their strange spell,
Excepting one, who knew it well.

—Brangaene, she, the prudent maid,
With her looks often strayed
Watchful toward the loving pair,
Noting their secret ways and care ;
And often to herself she thought :
" Alas that I this evil wrought !

Love in these two beginneth now."
Not long after she saw how
In both an eager earnestness,
Violent grief and strange distress
Of the heart and of the mind
Did outward expression find.
Then did their great grief cause her woe,
Whom she all times saw suffer so;
Ameiring and amuring,
Longingly enduring,
Yearning, thinking, falt'ring,
And their color alt'ring.
So mighty was their yearning :
Food and drink spurning,
They wasted, until want and care
Betrayed even by their bodies were ;
And Brangaene, the faithful maid,
Daily became more afraid
Death would on them both lay hold.
" Now let me be quick and bold,"
Spoke she, " and ask their secret grame."

— Then there sat one day with them
Quietly watching
The proud, wise maid — catching
Quick at the chance : " Here is none but us three,
Now tell me, what is't with you two ? " said she.
" Every hour in pensive mood
You sit here and sigh and brood,
Listless, drooping and complain."
" Lady, dared I but explain

I'd gladly do it," said Tristan.
" But sir, that dare you well ; come, then,
Tell me, what it is you crave ? "
" Blessed maid," reply then gave
Tristan, " I dare not say more,
Unless you solemnly before
With oath pledge us assurance,
That you to us two poor ones
Will graciously assistance give,
For otherwise we may not live."

— Brangaene quickly pledged her word.
She promiscd her mistress and her lord,
With oaths, that even unto death
To their behests she'd plight her faith.
Then Tristan said : "Thou good and kind,
First on God direct your mind,
Then consult your own goodness,
Consider our grievous distress
And all our suffering untold.
I, poor one, and the poor Isolde —
How it has come, I know not ; — we
Within short time have grown to be
Crazy both of us sadly ;
Suffering strangely and madly.
We're dying in love's fever,
And yet cannot find ever
Chance or occasion.
'Tis you who disturbs our passion.
And should we die, most 'suredly
You alone the cause would be.
Our life and death even

Into your hands are given.
Herewith now enough is said,
Brangaene, blessed maid,
Help us and save us graciously,
Isolde, your lady, as well as me."

— Brangaene to Isolde spoke :
"Lady, has this passion's yoke,
As he doth say, on you such hold ? "
"Aye, heart's cousin," said Isolde.
Brangaene cried : "God rue the day
That the devil thus his play
With us three has carried on.
I see well, nothing can now be done ;
For you I must offer,
Howe'er loth, to suffer
E'en disgrace and shame ; for I,
Rather than to let you die,
Will give you opportunity.
What you to do may willing be,
For my sake leave it not undone,
If you for honor and duty alone
Do not choose to shun it.
But could you leave undone it,
And to do't yourselves restrain,
Then to restrain I'd urge again.
At least the shame concealed let be,
And closely kept between us three.
If you keep not the story,
'Twill cost you fame and glory.
Unless you keep it close, you two,
I shall be lost, and so shall you.

Dear heart's lady, sweet Isolde,
Your life as well as death you hold
Into your own hands given.
Now death and life guide even
As in your heart you are inclined.
Henceforth never more you'll find
Me a hindrance to you two ;
Whate'er you please to do, that do."

When the lady lay alone that night,
Grieving and suffering, in sore plight
For her friend and lover,
Then did stealthily hover
Nearer to her casemate's side,
Her friend, her doctress and her bride :
Love, her Tristan leading,
Love, for Tristan pleading ;
With her sufferer at her side,
Tristan, who for love sheer died.
Love found another sufferer there.
The sufferers then love took with care,
And gave her him and him to her,
Each the other's cure fore'er.
What else, indeed, could ever
These two in this world sever
From their same grief and union,
Than common sweet communion,
And entrancement of their feeling ?
Entrancing Love, full willing,
So caught the maid's heart and eke his
With the trances of its great sweetness,
With such a mighty master skill,

With such a wonderful power and will,
That it held them forever ;
Redeemèd they were never.

And now, after all this tumult of passion, how exquisitely does the poet improve the pause for the
thoughtful lines that follow : —

— For love with long speech pleading
Offendeth courtly breeding :
Short speech for good love pleading,
Doeth good to goodly breeding.

— However little in my life
Of love I've suffered and love's strife,
That gentle heart-love's smarting,
Which, in the heart upstarting,
So mickle gently ungentle stirs ;
Yet my mind to me avers,
And joyful am I to believe :
These two lovers felt relief,
And happy and blessed were amain
When they knew shame's hated bane,
That torture of true loving,
Love's enemy removing,
And from their path wending away.
I have thought much of both alway,
And think to-day and all the days,
When love and yearning heart's distress
Before my eyes outspreading,
I 'gin their various pleading

In heart and thought to ponder.
Lo! then my soul with wonder
And courage, my heart's comrade, swells:
High in the clouds it mounts and dwells.
When I still further ponder
This wonder and that wonder,
Which he, who knew how't to detect
In love could find and from't extract;
The joy by love to be spended,
If faithfully attended:
My heart so big within me grows,
The whole wide world it overflows.
And pities me love dearly!
My heart is touchèd nearly,
In that the most of living men
Around love rally and wear its chain,
Whilst none of them love justly treat.
We all would like things so to fit
As to make a friend of this same love.
But love does not so act and move
As we t'ourselves keep doing:
With false pretense and showing.
We take an unjust view of things:
We sow the seed that henbane brings;
And then expect that this vile seed
Roses and lilies us should breed.
In faith, but this can never be.
We must expect to reap as we
Into the ground have put before;
Must take that which the seed us bore.
We must cut and we must mow
Even as we erst did sow.

We would build love's dwelling,
Our heart with bile o'erswelling,
With falsity and with a lie,
And then search in't to find true joy
Of heart and body; O folly!
It brings us troubles solely,
Bad mood, bad fruit, and bad lot,
Just as we in the building put.
Now when repentance there doth rise
And into our heart its poison flies,
Our life within us strangling,
We charge love with wrangling,
And accuse't of that which ne'er
Love was guilty of putting there.
We do always falseness sow;
Then vice and sorrow for us grow.
If the sorrow us sore does touch,
We ought to consider much,
How to do better sowing;
Then might come better mowing
We who have a worldly mood,
Whether 'tis evil or whether good:
How do we spend our days?
We dissipate them in many ways
Under love's name's cover,
And find them all over.
Bring forth nought but the same work,
Which we to put there did not shirk:
Miscarryings and mishap.
We find ne'er that good in'ts lap,
For which each of us here pines,
And which yet no one entwines:

Namely, a steady friend's kind mood,
With gentleness steadily imbued,
Which roses with the thorns e'er brings,
Which fanneth labor with rest's sweet wings,
Wherein lies hid in a furrow,
Love close unto sorrow,
Which every end with joy doth crown,
As often as it was outthrown.
Ah, little do we now of't find:
Such fruit our works have borne in kind.

— 'Tis mickle true that which they say:
"Love has been driven and chased away;
To the furthest end of the world't has soared."
We've only left of it the word.
Us is remained nought but the name.
And e'en that we've so driven to shame,
So wrong-worded, and so wrong-named,
That love out of its name is shamed;
And from the word gets trouble.
Love seems t'itself a bubble,
A sickened thing upon the earth.
Honorless and without worth
It sneaks 'long the houses begging;
And like the vicious goes dragging
A many-folded bag along,
Wherein its stolen things are flung.
Thus love itself slays in the face,
And offers itself in public ways.
Ah woe! such market we have made!
Such change must to our doors be laid;
And yet we all claim innocence!

Love, the queen of every man's
Heart and soul, the holy,
Is open to purchase solely.
Lordly domain we held in her,
Now are we wretched renters mere.
We have a wicked counterfeit
Put in her gold ring — such a cheat,
Wherewith ourselves we're cheating.
A cheat, so badly fitting,
That while it cheats our friends, it aye
Comes back and cheats us the same way.
We miserable love-cheaters !
We love's false counterfeiters !
How do our days from us so pass,
That to this straying in wickedness
We put an end so rarely !
How passes our life, so sparely
Endowed with pleasure and with good !
And yet it gives us pleasant mood
When in another field it grows.
Whate'er fine story is told to us
Of matters of love affections,
All speeches we hear of the actions
Of those who lived before us, lo
Many hundred years ago :
This in our hearts gives us good cheer,
And this mood does so many stir,
That rarely lived one ever,
Who truthfulness did favor,
And who to friend ne'er falseness bore,
But such a cheer would o'er and o'er

15

In heart and sense keep trying
To rouse sincere enjoying.
But lo, most pitifully it
In wretchedness now lies 'neath our feet,
It, that such joy in us does move :
The truth and steadfastness of love !
In vain it offers itself to us.
Our eyes we turn away, and thus
The sweetest one we shatter
Under our feet and scatter.
We have trodden her out of worth
Into the dust of the earth ·
Now, should we go to hunt the place,
We'd scarcely find it out straightways.
But since such very sweet reward
This faithfulness for us does guard,
Why then do we love it not ?
A glance from face that loveth, caught
From eyes that heart-love treasure,
Can drown in fullest measure
Hundred thousand sorrows,
That heart or body borrows.
A kiss from lips love-rounded,
If from the heart it bounded
And upward ventured daftly ;
Ah me ! how quickly and softly
It would dispel all heart's distress !

As a further and final specimen of Gottfried's art,
we give the description of Tristan and Isolde's life in
the " Grotto of Love." Let the reader compare with
it the treatment of the same subject under the hands

of all other poets, particularly of Gottfried's contemporaries and predecessors, the French poets, and he cannot but admire the free grace, ingenuity, and chaste art-spirit with which Gottfried has wrought out the same. The latter part contains, as it were, the *apologia* of the whole poem.

With this extract we must take leave of the poem, and indeed of the whole subject. Perhaps it would have been more interesting to sketch out the story itself as Gottfried has told it, but as he remains generally faithful to the well-known features of the legend, it seemed more useful to present the workmanship of the artist by a translation of two of the finest parts of his work.

The lovers have just been turned out of court by King Mark, who has finally made up his mind that they are guilty, though he has never been able to get conclusive proof. Brangaene is sent along with them, and the three proceed thus into the wilderness.

TRISTAN AND ISOLDE IN THE GROTTO OF LOVE.

Thus went the three with steady pace
Onward to the wilderness,
Through forest and o'er heather
Full two days together.
There Tristan knew from long ago
In a wild mountain a cave lying low,
Which he had found when faring
On some venture daring.
He had been riding upon his horse,
And chance had made him take this course.

This same cave had long before
In the heathen times of yore,
Ere Korineus was master,
When giants ruled, spreading disaster,
In the mountain's side been cut.
There had they had their hiding-spot,
When in secret they would be
And worship love's mystery.
Where such a cave their sight allured
With iron they had it secured,
And by Love's name 'mongst them it went:
La fossiure u la gont amant:
Which meaneth e'en: the Grotto of Love.
And fitting, too, the name does prove.
The story tells, moreover,
Of this *fossiure* and cover,
As being wide, high, and upright,
Snow-white, everywhere even and tight.
The vaulted roof closed tightly,
Deserving all praise ; and brightly
Upon the joint great splendor
A pendent crown did render,
Adorned all o'er and under
With gems : a jeweled wonder !
And down below the floor did stretch ;
Smooth, and pure, and very rich,
Of green marble, e'en as grass.
A bed in the middle had its place,
Finely upon its pedestal
Cut out of pure crystal ;
High and wide, well upraised,
With letters on each side skillfully traced.

Further the story has noted :
The grotto was devoted
To the Goddess of Love.
In the grotto, ranged above,
Little windows had been made
Where the light came in and played.
These gave light here and there.
Where you went in and out, there were
The fastenings of an iron door.
Outside stood, the door before,
Richly-branched lindens three ;
None more above these could you see ;
But everywhere else around
Countless trees were to be found,
To all the mountains' ranges
Giving shade with leaves and branches.
Within the plain of the mountain
Played a flowing fountain,
With fresh clear life inherent,
And as the sun transparent.
Around it, too, three linden stood,
Beautiful, worthy of praise, and good,
Sheltering the river
From rain and sunshine ever.
Glowing flowers and green-sheened grass,
Wherewith the plain all lit up was,
Battled e'er so sweetly there.
Each one seemed there but to care
How to outdo the other's glows.
In proper time there too arose
The pretty birds' sweet ditty ;
Their ditty rang there as pretty,

Aye, prettier than anywhere.
Eyes and ears as well had there
Rapture both and pleasure:
The eye its pleasure could treasure,
The ear its passing rapture.
Shade and sun there you could capture;
And air and wind played meetly
There forever sweetly.
From this mountain and cave away
About the distance of a day,
Lay rocky ground and hilly,
A desert wild and chilly;
There no opportunity
Of way or path the eye could see.
Yet was there nought so dreary
In this wild place, or weary,
But Tristan there must now
With his loved companion go,
Taking up quarters by the fountain
In the rocks and in the mountain.

Now when they'd quartered there, the twain,
They sent Kurvenal again,
News at the court to be spreading,
And where he might deem't needing,
That Tristan and the fair Isolde
In misery and woes manifold,
Passage had taken for Ireland's shore,
There their innocence all o'er
To make known to men and land.
They told him to depart off-hand
And at the court be ready

To do whate'er the lady
Brangaene might command him,
And to do remand him,
In her love unremitting
For both ; her troth ne'er quitting.
They told him also to find out
What King Mark might be about,
Whether he had not wicked mind
Some wickedness to do, and find
If Mark inclined to kill them ;
Then quick to come and tell them.
Again their messenger they told
Ever Tristan and Isolde
To remember duly,
And return most truly
With news that he might gather,
As ought to be known to either,
Once in every twenty days.
What more need I now digress ?
He did e'en as he was told.
Thus were Tristan and Isolde
In their house unnettled
Within this wilderness settled.

Now many a one does ponder,
And here has mickle wonder,
Greatly distressed e'en to be told
How Tristan and Isolde
Managed themselves to nourish
In this desert, and not to perish.
This now will I e'en tell them
And their great doubts dispel them :

They looked into each other's face;
Thus their nourishing took place.
The fullness, which the eye filled o'er,
Was their nourishment and store.
Nought else was now their eating
But love and soul's sweet greeting.
This loving *massenie*
Was their only *mangerie;*
It gave them little trouble.
Under their dress the couple
Sweetly concealed did carry
Food the best, most cheery,
Which in the world can e'er be got.
This of itself to them it brought,
New and fresh each ration.
'Twas even pure troth's passion,
Love, th' embalmed and holy,
Which body and soul so fully
Fills with inmost gentleness;
Which lends to heart and soul its grace;
This was there their best nourishment.
Seldom they e'er their pleasure bent
To any other food than this,
Of which the heart drew all its bliss
And the eye its ecstasy;
E'en with the body't did agree,
Thereof had they enough I trow.
Love steadily pulled its plow,
Following them step by step,
At every hour, through every hap,
And gave them all in fullest flow
That for well living life needs bestow.

Nor caused it them heart-burning,
That, into the desert turning,
They were left so all alone.
What needed they any other one,
Or should they do with company?
They were an even number; see,
There were simply one and one.
What should there a third have done?
Had he joined their number even,
It uneven had turned and given,
By this same uneveness
Them but trouble and distress.
To these two their society
Seemed in the twain so grand and free,
That the blessèd Arthur ne'er
At home, in his own house, such cheer
And wondrous feast did enjoy,
As could have made them think't more high
And richer in its pleasures.
Of bliss, no joyful measures
Could have been found in any land,
For which these two, thus hand in hand,
Coupled and blessed together,
Had given the blow of a feather.

What every one would surely call
The happiest, sweetest life of all
In any country, far or near,
They had in the forest here.
For better life they even
Would not a bean have given,
'Twere then their honor to regain.
Indeed, what more could they attain?

They had a court and wealth no less
Which surely giveth happiness.
Their ample court and their wide hall
Were the linden green and tall,
The sunshine and the shadow,
The spring and the meadow,
Grass, flowers, leaves, and blossom,
What gladdens the eye and the bosom.
Their servants were the songs of the vale :
The little, gentle nightingale,
The graceful linnet and the thrush,
And other birdlets of the bush.
The goldfinch and the lark so dear
Sang against each other here,
As in zealous rivalry.
These servants always served in glee
Their senses and their hearing.
Their feast was love endearing.
Love, the crown of all their joy,
So to charm both in heart and eye
At every hour was able,
That Arthur's Round Table
And all its joys they here did feel.
Needed they any better meal?
Or cheer more sweetly human?
Here was man with woman
And woman with man :
What more needed they, then?
They had what they ought to,
And never where they sought to.
Yet many still will worry
And with their speech us flurry,

Although I will not follow them,
Who say this play needs all the same
Ever other kind of food.
I know not if this speech be good,
For still methinks that does suffice.
But if another man, more wise,
Better food than that one
Ever in his life has known,
Let him speak as he knows it.
I, too, to lead once chose it,
Made that mode of life my own ;
Then thought I't food enough alone.

Now let me keep your favor
As I t'explain endeavor
My meaning when I asserted
The *fossiure,* where they consorted,
Had the form as I have told.
It was, as I did erst unfold,
Rounded, wide, high, and upright,
Snow-white, everywhere even and tight.
The vault so rounded riven
Is love's simplicity even.
Simplicity fits well love's shape,
For love should have no cornered trap.
The corner, which is found in love,
Is falsity and cunning's groove.
The wideness love's power does portend,
For love's power is without an end.
The height is e'en of love th' high mood,
Which up in the clouds e'er seeks its flood ;
For it deems nought ever too high,
Since it would rise up to that sky

Where all the virtues join and dwell
Together in a vaulted spell,
Nor knows it ever failing.
Those virtues are impaling,
Bejeweled and besplendored,
With glory so engendered,
That we, whose mood tendeth but low,
Whose mood doth ever downward flow
And keepeth clinging to the floor,
Neither floating, nor sticking more:
We all do ever upward look
And contemplate that glorious book,
Whereon those virtues are writ in gold,
Where from their praise pours down unrolled,
Which over us in the clouds float bright,
And stream adown to us their light:
These look we at with wond'ring gaze;
These grow us wings by their sweet grace,
That waft the mood to that clear height,
Where praises it draws from them in its flight.

The wall was white, even and tight;
This is truthfulness, e'er bright.
Its whiteness and its self-same sheen
Never must be speckled seen.
Nor must on't suspicion find
Cracks or spots of any kind.
The marble floor, that outspread there,
To steadfastness we may compare
In firmness and green splendor;
This it does visible render

In color and in quality,
For steadfastness ought e'er to be
E'en as green as the grass,
And as polished and pure as glass.
The bed, in the middle framèd,
Crystal Love was namèd,
And most justly this name bore.
He love's rights knew o'er and o'er
Who from crystal had it made
For love's resting-place and bed,
Since love, like crystal, must abide
Transparent and transpurified.

Inside on the iron door
Two bolts were put before ;
A latch there also fastened,
Skillfully wrought in the best, and
Made to pass to the outer side ;
Where Tristan found it to abide.
This outside knob a lever moved,
From the outside to the inside grooved,
And thus the door opened and shut ;
No lock nor key in it was put.
And I will tell you why this was :
There was no lock to the door because
Whatever fastening on a door,
I mean on th' outside and no more,
To close it or to lock't is made
Tends all to show there 's falseness laid.
For who would enter the door of love
When't does not from inside open move,

He follows not love's own true course,
But uses falseness and vile force.
For this 'tis, that love's gate before
You always find the iron door,
Which none can hope to be moving,
Unless they move't with loving.
'Tis also iron, mark ye that,
That no force can be connived at,
Neither of violence or ill
Of cunning or of master-skill,
Or falsehood that could copen
With the door and force it open.
And inward each bolt, fastened,
Each bolt love's own seal chastened,
Was each one toward the other bent;
Toward either side of the wall they went;
And one was made of the cedar tree,
And the other one of ivory.
Now their portend consider:
The seal made of cedar
Proves that love enhances
Wisdom and the senses.
The ivory shows with sureness
Love's chastity and pureness.
With these two seals well warded,
With these pure bolts well guarded,
Is ever kept the house of love;
Force nor lie can into't move.

The knob, of which I spoke before,
Which from th' outside through the door,
Was led the latch to catch,

Was a knob of tin ; the latch
Itself of gold wrought neatly,
As it should be fitly.
Latch and knob, this and that,
Neither could have had better mate,
Or in a better way been wrought.
The tin portends the will and thought
In secret to pursue it.
The gold is, how to do it.
Tin and gold fit well in here :
His will each man can certainly steer
As he chooses, and guiden,
Narrow it or widen,
Shorten or lengthen,
Weaken or strengthen,
Thus or thus, this or that way,
With little labor, like tin bends aye,
And without harm to't being done.
But who with kindly will alone
On love has bent his heart and thought,
This little knob of tin has brought, —
This tin, unseemly treasure, —
Near golden joy and pleasure,
And most rare adventure.

In the cave indenture
Was only by three windows made ;
Nicely and secretly too they had
Through the mountain's rock been cut :
Through them the sunshine came to the spot.
The one is kind behavior,
The other meekness' favor,

The third propriety.   To these three
Laugheth in the sweet glow free,
The ever-blessèd honor,
Of all the best light-donor ;
And lights up all the places
Of blessed adventure and graces.
'T had also meaning surely,
That the *fossiure* demurely
Lay in the wilderness alone.
From it this simile may be won :
That love and love's chance are not free
Offered on streets and publicly,
Nor in open spaces.
Love lieth in wild, strange places ;
T'her home the path is dreary,
Laborsome, and weary.
Mountains lie around it,
And with many a turning bound it,
Leading astray the seekers.
Paths up and down, with breakers,
For us poor martyrs groping,
And rocks bestrewn run sloping,
So twistedly, keep we not straight
On the path, or but one step stray get,
We ne'er shall find a clearing,
But stay there ever erring.
But who so blessèd shall be found
That he at last reaches its bound,
That same one all his toil's distress
Most blessedly invested has.
There findeth he his heart's loved play ;
For what the ear would hear alway,
And what the eye should ever love,

All in this wilderness does move,
He would not like to be elsewhere.

This I know well, for I was there.
I also in this hollow
Wild birds and game did follow ;
The stag and wild beasts over
Many a wooded cover
Following and pursuing ;
But yet time so undoing,
That I the quarry[1] ne'er saw yet.
My labor and my toil ne'er met
Any sort of adventure.
I found the *fossiure's* centre,
The knob and latch I lifted.
Yea, to the crystal drifted
I at hours and eyed it,
Often and often I tried it,
E'en how to reach it, drawing close,
Yet did I ne'er in it repose.
Ah, but the floor in front of it !
However hard its marble sheet,
I so with steps have it defaced :
Had not its greenness food replaced,
From which it all its virtues drew,
Of which it daily anew there grew,
You still could see engraven
The trace Love's steps had paven.
Aye, and of the gleaming wall
Often did my eyes scan all ;

[1] Skinning of the deer.

16

And all o'er the vaulted dome
Where the arches together come
Have I glanced with wonder.
My eyes opened to yonder
Jeweled crown so fairly
Bestarred, praiseworthy and rarely.
The sun-erasing window's art
Even has sent into my heart
Often their brightest glow.
I this *fossiure* learned to know
Even at my eleventh year ;
And yet in Kurnerval was I ne'er.

The faithful and devoted pair,
Tristan and Isolde the fair,
Had in this sweet wilderness,
The forest and the fields, sweet ease
And time enough to ponder,
And o'er their love to wonder.
They both loved ever and alway
At each other's side to stay.
At morning in the dew they went
Down to the meadow's wide extent,
Whereon the grass and colored flowers
Stood new-refreshed by dewy showers.
The cool fresh meadow there did seem
A fairy realm of bliss to them.
Together up and down they'd walk
Talking together sweet love-talk ;
And listening 'midst their whispered words
To the sweet singing of the birds.
Then would they walk towards a spot

Where a cool spring played in a grot ;
To its sweet tune then list'ning,
And watching it flowing and glist'ning
To where it vanished in the plain.
There sat they down and rested then,
List'ning to the flowing,
And watching the rivulet's glowing :
This was their sweetest pleasure.

But when the sun's full measure
Began to show itself on high,
And fiercer heat fell from the sky,
Then went they to the shadow
Of the linden on the meadow,
Where the sweet breezes still their breast
Both in and outwardly caressed ;
They gladdened their eye and senses there.
There the sweet linden sweetened e'er
By its green leaves the air and shade.
Its shade the gentle wind sweet made :
Sweet, cool, and refreshing.
The linden's bench was flashing
With flowers and grass so gay, I wot,
It made it the best-painted spot
That e'er did round a linden stand.
And here they sat them, hand in hand,
Lover by faithful lover,
Telling old stories over
Of passionate lovers, that, years ago,
Were all destroyed by love's great woe.
They talked of many a lover ;
Pitying and sorrowing over

Phyllis of Thracia and her fate,
And poor Canacé, and the great
Anguish she suffered from love's stroke.
And o'er sweet Byblis, whose heart broke
With love for her fair brother.
Then wept they o'er that other
Sad tale of Dido, Queen of Tyre
And Sidon, who from love's wild fire
Had suffered sorrows great and sore.
Thus beguiled they with love-lore
Many an hour of leisure.
When then they felt a pleasure
Another sport or joy to have,
They'd retire into their cave
And there take into their hand
Whatsoever mirth might lend.
Then through the cave went ringing
Their harping and their singing
Yearningly and sweetly.
They changed their playing fitly
With their hands and their tongue.
Thus they harped and they sung
Lays and notes of loving.
Therein they kept moving
As it might please either one.
Whiche'er then struck the harp's sweet tone
It ever was the other's way
To deem't so sweet and fine a play
That th' other needs must sing thereto.
Moreover ev'ry sound there so
Delightfully and sweetly rung
Of the harp and of the tongue,

When they joined in a harmony,
That their cave most truthfully
Ever by the sweet name went:
La fossiure a la gent amant.
But all that of adventure
Round this *fossiure* did centre,
And ever had been spoken,
Of that got they full token.
Their hostess, Love, that treasure,
Now first began her pleasure
In that cavern to display.
Whate'er had been before that day
Of games invented or delights,
Came not up to their new rites.
Of love was livèd surely
Never aught so purely
Than amongst them their loving play.
They passed love's hours away so gay,
So well, as never lovers did.
Naught but whercunto they were bid
By their own hearts did they ever do.

Enough of pastime found the two
T'indulge in each day's courses.
They rode at times on horses
Through the wildernesses
With their arching pieces;
O'er the desert prying,
Birds and wild beasts spying.
Some days too adown the hollow
In the chase the stag they'd follow
With Hiudane, their faithful hound,
That ne'er before was known to bound

Without bark the track anent.
But Tristan now so'd trained its scent,
And taught it over and over
To follow the deer, or the cover
Of the wild beast, or any game,
Through forests and through fields the same,
On the scent of the beast,
Without bark or noise the least.
Therewith enjoyed they many a day ;
Nor did they do it for the prey
As most men do it in the chase.
They did it for pastime always,
And always found it them to please.
Their hound and eke their arching piece
They exercised, as I well know,
More for their pleasure and heart's glow,
And for delectation,
Than to seek their ration.
Their doings and their passions
Were upon all occasions
Nothing else than simply this :
To do that which seemed most to please.

But the while this happened here,
Much distress and little cheer
Had King Mark, the weary.
He was mickle dreary
Over his honor and his wife.
Him now grew his mood and life
From day to day more cheerless,
Honor and good more dearless.
Now one day that time he rode

Out hunting in that self-same wood
More his grief to quiet
Than for venturous riot.
And when to the wood they came
They found there a herd of game
By their hounds' faithful scent.
Then the hounds forward went,
And the king's dogs with cunning art
Had quickly set and driven apart
From the herd a rare, strange stag.
A mane of horse flew from his neck ;
Strong was he and tall and sleek,
Small his horns, and antlered weak,
Just beginning regrowing,
As he'd been them off-throwing
Not so very long ago.
Him the chase hunted now
With a roused up rival zest
Till the eve set in at last ;
Then they were thrown off the track.
Thus the stag escaped and back
Hurried frightened to his home,
Even to where he had come from ;
This was where the *fossiure* was ;
Thither he fled and thus found grace.

Now worried it Mark sorely,
The hunters, too, felt poorly,
That it so happened with the deer.
For he had looked quite strange and queer
In his color and with his mane.
They all were disappointed then.

Their hounds they called back with all might ;
Then settled down to pass the night,
For rest they sorely needed all.
Now Tristan and Isolde the call
Of horns and hounds had the whole day
Heard coming through the forest aye,
The bugle and the barking ;
And had been remarking
Straightway that it must be Mark.
Then their hearts grew drear and dark.
Both were troubled by the fear,
He knew them concealèd here.

The next day at early dawn
The hunting master rose alone
Ere the clouds were lined with red,
And bid his men stay where they laid
Till the day's in the hollow,
Then his traces to follow.
To a leading string he tied
The surest hound that he espied,
And took him straight to the scent.
Then led the hound him as he went
Through many dangerous passes
O'er rocky and steep places,
Over stones and grassy plot
Till they came to the same spot,
Where last night the stag escaped.
Now followed they the trail, and trapped
Him through the hollow and the close ;
Then the morning sun arose
And found them on the mountain
E'en by Tristan's fountain.

That same early morn Tristan
And his love-companion,
Hand in hand walking,
Went forth, sweetly talking,
In th' early dew to the flowered
Meadow, where it lowered
Down into the glorious vale.
Lark and nightingale
Began their organ-fluting
Their company saluting.
They greeted, not unholdy,
Tristan and Isolde.
The wild birdlets of the wood
Bid them welcome too, renewed,
In their sweet-toned Latin.
Many sweet birds, their matin
Singing, found them welcome there.
They all had put on cheery air
Of pleasantest enjoyment.
To please, by their employment,
The loving twain, they sang now
Their blissful song, and rang now
Its changeful, varying measures.
O! many sweet tongue rare treasures
Then *schantoit* and *discantoit*,
In *schanzun* and in *refloit*
For the lovers' hearing.
The cool spring endearing
Most sweetly shone on their sight, and dear,
But sweeter still rang in their ear.
Murmuring't went to greet the pair,
And with its murmur received them there.

Sweetly it murmured, fitting
Gentle lover's greeting.
The linden too greeting uttered
With sweet winds, low-fluttered,
Inward and outward enticing,
The ears and the heart rejoicing.
The wood-trees blossom
The meadows gay bosom,
The flowers, and the dark green grass,
And all that blooming around there was,
It all laughed at them sweetest smile.
Sweet greeting e'en did round them coll,
The dew's fresh fullness.
It gave their feet coolness
And refreshed their heart and soul.

When this had been done to the full,
They stole to the grotto back,
And began counsel to take
How to guide their doing,
For fears kept them pursuing,
And dread — e'en as it came to be —
That in some way soon somebody
Of the hunters might pass by them
And in their doings spy them.
Then hit Tristan on a thought,
Which pleased both and was done on the spot.
They went into the bed again
And there again laid down, the twain,
But apart, in such a way
As a man with man does lay,
Not as woman with a man.

Thus lay love with love, but fain
In strange fashion in the bed.
Tristan furthermore had laid
His naked sword between the pair ;
Thus lay he here and she lay there ;
They lay asunder, one and one ;
Thus asleep together gone.

The hunter now, of whom I read,
Whom to the spring his hound had led,
Saw in the dew some traces,
E'en Tristan and Isolde's paces,
Where they had gone before that day.
These took he for the stag's lost way,
He jumped from horse and 'gan to take
Straight along the self-same track
Which the two had gone before.
This brought him to the *fossiure's* door,
But this securely had been shut
By the two bolts behind it put :
So now no further could he go.
But since this path was closed t'him so,
He tried to get around it.
All round and round he found it
Tightly closed, until by chance
Up above espied his glance
A concealèd window neat.
Cautiously looked he into it
And beheld, thus spying,
Love's sole guests there lying :
Simply a woman and a man.
Wondrously he looked again,

For to him seemed the woman
So fair, as ne'er of common
Woman's womb, so rarely made,
Into the world could have been bred.
Yet did he not a long while stare
Until his eyes became aware
How the sword there naked laid.
Thereat became he sore afraid,
It seemed to him quite frightening.
He thought he might be sightening
Some unearthly things in the cave.
Fear drove him himself to save :
He ran quick down the mountain
And back to the hound by the fountain.

Now Mark had also hastened,
And, his horse unfastened,
In advance of his followers, rode through the wood.
He met that hunter as he rode.
" O, listen! " cried he, panting,
" King, Lord, I bring enchanting
News of rare adventure,
Which here around does centre."
" Adventure ?   Of what manner ? "
" A Love-fossiure ! "   " Speak plainer !
Where didst thou find it, in what way ? "
" My Lord, e'en in this wold astray."
" In this wild desert wold ? "   " Sire, yes ! "
" Is any one living in the place ? "
"Yes, sir, it is the cover
Of a goddess and man lover,
Upon a bed they're sleeping

As if a wager keeping.
The man is like another man,
But I some doubts do still retain
Whether his sleep comrade be
A human being : so fair is she.
Aye, fairer than a fairy.
Of flesh and bone, unairy,
Could ne'er have been bred creature
On earth, so shaped each feature.
And, — I know not from what cause, —
A naked sword between them was
Lying, very bright and gay."
The king said, " Lead thou me the way."

Then led the hunter him again
Through the wilderness and plain
To where he erst dismounted had.
The king dismounted too, and bade
The hunter stay e'en where he was ;
Alone the king strode through the grass.
And now when Mark came to the door,
He turned aside and o'er and o'er
The cavern's walls went spying,
Each side of the stone walls trying,
And taking every turning
He from the hunter'd been learning,
Till he came to the windowed place.
Then through the window fell his gaze
On love and sorrow, sweet couple.
He saw them both so supple
Moulded lying there in the bed
Of crystal, still in deep sleep laid.

He found them, too, as they had been found,
Each from the other turned around,
The one this way, the other that,
Between them the drawn sword lay pat.
He recognized nephew and wife ;
His heart within him, yea, all his life
Turned cold with infinite loving,
Aye, and with sorrow moving.
This strange opportunity
Woke both pleasure and sorrow, see :
Pleasure, as attesting
Their innocence, thus resting ;
Sorrow, to see together both.
In his heart spoke he loth :
" Gracious God and Lord, show me
What may the truth of these things be ?
If anything like that has passed,
Which my suspicion charged amazed,
How lie they in this fashion ?
Sure woman loved man with passion
Should in her arms be holding,
Always dearly enfolding,
How then these lovers lie they so ? "
Then to himself spoke he low :
" In this matter is there aught ?
Is there guilt or is there not ? "
Thus came doubt with sore distress.
" Guilt ? " said he, " Truly, yes."
" Guilt ? " said he, " Truly, no ! "

Thus ruminated he on the two,
Till the poor way-lost man,

Mark, at last to doubt began
Of the lovers' loving.
Love, e'er hate-removing,
Stole moreo'er unto him
Assurance full to show him,
Adorned in all her brightness.
She had on her whiteness
Skillfully spread over
Bold lie's red gold cover,
Painted in best color: No!
This word shone and cast its glow
Into Mark's heart most thorough.
The other, his great sorrow,
The word, so mickle unpleasant, Yes,
Of that saw Mark now not the least trace.
It had straightway been put aside,
No doubt or fear did now abide.
Love's own overguilding maid,
Sweet golden Innocence, now led
His eyes and soul and senses
With her coaxing trances
To where the gladsome easterday,
Aye, of all his pleasures lay.
He looked upon that treasure,
Isolde, his heart's sole pleasure,
And never in all past time't did seem
So beautiful had she looked to him.

I know not what toil't could have been,
Which could have heated her rosy sheen
As the story telleth us,
Coloring her so glorious,

She seemed so sweetly burning
A mixèd rose upturning
Her wondrous face up to the man.
Her mouth fired and burned again
Even as a burning coal.
Ah, now I recollect the whole
What the toil was made it so.
Isolde, I said not long ago,
Had in the dew of the morning
Down to the dale been turning,
And this had roused her color.
The sun, too, risen fuller,
Now down upon her sent a gleam,
Upon her cheek lit the wee stream,
And on her mouth and on her chin.
Two wonders joined that time to win
Between themselves a curious game ;
Light and light shone ; both the same ;
This sun and that sun ; either
Had great joy together
In the wedding, they thus play'd
On Isolde's face upon her bed.
Her chin, her mouth, her color, her skin
Shone, O, so wondrous there within,
So lovingly, so full of grace ;
Mark felt it rushing to his face ;
Desire arose and yearning
To kiss that mouth love-burning.
Love came and threw in him her flame,
Love threw her flames in the man so grame,
By the beauty of her body.
Her beauty so sunny and ruddy

Coaxed with all its trances
To love and loving his senses.
His eye looked with a charmèd stare,
Deeply he became aware
How beautiful gleamed from her dress
Her neck and her bosom's grace,
Her arms and hands so rounded.
Her hair, all unbounded,
Had upon't a clover-wreath.
Her master thought her — scarce did he breathe —
More charming than she ever was.

Now when he saw the sunshine, as
It from above through the stone
Upon her glorious features shone,
He feared that her complexion might
Be harmed and damaged by the light.
He took grass, flowers, leaves, and thus
The window he began to close.
Then wafting toward the fair his blessing,
And for her welfare God addressing,
He took leave, weeping amain.
The broken-hearted man again
To his hounds returnèd straight.
The chase he stopped, nor did he wait,
But speedily commanded,
The hunt being ended,
Hunters and hounds home to return.
This did he, that no one might learn
About the grotto and go there
And behold the banished pair.

17

Scarce had the king departed when
Isolde woke up and Tristan.
Now when they 'gan to look around
For the sunshine, lo, they found
It shone not in as it did before,
But only through two windows more.
When then they looked up to the third,
And saw no light through it appeared,
They began to wonder.
Nor waited they longer yonder
But straightway got up both and took
Outside of the cave good look.
Then leaves, flowers, and the grass
Which were in the window's place
To their sight appeared off-hand.
The two traced also in the sand
Of the *fossiure* and far back
A man's step and a man's track,
Even there and even then.
This made tremble them again
And with fear to flurry.
They thought in their worry
Mark had somehow found the spot
And of them had taken note.
This their apprehension was ;
But of certainty no trace
Could they there discover.
Their great hope was moreover,
That whosoe'er had seen them
Had seen the sword between them,
And how they turned from each other were,
And in what manner lying there.

The king at once 'gan sending
And bid at court attending
All the counsel and friends of his
T'advise with them in his distress.
He told them and made to them known,
All I just to you have shown ;
How he had found the couple,
And how, 'midst all his trouble,
He had resolved that he would hold
Guiltless both Tristan and Isolde.
His counsel noted them off hand
How his will now seemed to bend,
And that his speech was even framed
To have the fair to the court reclaimed.
They counseled as the wise men do,
That is, e'en as his heart did show,
And as his wishes tended :
That he should send befriended
Messenger to his nephew and wife ;
No proof of guilt or shameless life
Being had, and no suspicion raised,
Kurvenal was called and pressed
To undertake the passage
Through the wilderness with this message,
He knowing where to find them.
The king bid him remind them,
Both Tristan and his wife, the queen,
Of his love and grace, and e'en
Tell them on their returning
No more jealous heart-burning
Should ever trouble between them raise.

Kurvenal then went his ways
And to both made known Mark's mood.
This seemed to both the lovers good,
And in their hearts they both were glad.
This gladness through both of them had
In a far greater measure
For God and honor than pleasure,
Or for any other thing on earth.
Both returned to former worth
And their station as before.
But henceforth and nevermore
In all their years they ever
So sweetly quatted love's favor.
Nor found they opportunity
E'er as before that time, so free.
And yet King Mark endeavored,
And court and men all favored
To show them kindness still stronger.
But they were no longer
Free and constraintless.
Mark from doubt ne'er taintless
Entreated and commanded,
From Tristan and Isolde demanded,
That they for God's sake and for his
Should proper measure keep in this,
And the ever sweet trances
Of their loving glances
Try to avoid and smother.
Nor keep so near each other
And speak so lovingly as before.
This grieved the lovers very sore.

Mark, however, now was glad.
For his gladness, though, he had
In his wife, whatever
His heart desired of favor,
Only in appearance.
He had no endearance
Of love or of loving,
That happiness heart moving,
Which God created, in his wife.
True in his name and for his life
She was his lady and his queen.
In all that he was king within.
Yet did he take it all for good
And cherish toward her fond mood
As if he were her lover.
This was the fault all over
Of that heartless blindedness,
And foolish, whereof the proverb says :
" The blindness of love blindeth
Outward and inward ; and grindeth
Blindness out of eye and mind,
So that they'll never see and find
What yet before their sight lies close."
To Mark it happened even thus :
He knew it just as sure as death,
And saw how Isolde's his wife's faith
Heart and soul kept moving
Simply in Tristan's loving ;
How this to them was all ; but lo,
Although he saw he would not know.
Now whom shall we assign the guilt
Of that joyless life, unhealt,

The two led thus together?
For truly it were neither
Right nor fair to accuse Isolde
Of falseness or deceiving mould.
Nor she deceived him, nor Tristan.
With his own eyes he saw it plain
And knew it unseen well enough,
That she for him had ne'er felt love ;
And yet he loved her without that.
" But why, sir, tell us, and for what
Bore he towards her such loving mood?"
For the same cause, which yet holds good :
Desiring and love yearning
Must suffer heart-burning ;
For so to suffer is their fate.

Ah, how e'en yet to-day are met
So many a Mark and Isolde here —
But that they wish't not mentioned e'er! —
Who blinder or at least as blind
In heart and eye are, and in mind.
Not only are there not found none,
No, many and many are there, each one
With blindness struck so sheerly,
He will not know what clearly
Before his eyes lies patent.
His hope in a lie stays latent,
Although he knows, and though he sees.
Whose fault then is this blindness his?
If we would judge them fairly
The women should be clearly
Charged with no guilt ; for this is plain :

They're innocent towards the men,
Whom they let with their own eyes see
What they are doing openly.
Who sees the guilt with his own eyes
Cannot say that his wife him lies,
Cheats, or deceives. No, truly,
'Tis simply lust, th' unruly,
Which draws the neck up 'fore his eyes.
Lust is that cataract which lies
Blinding in the well-seeing sight
Of all the world and time and light.
Whatever men of blindness say:
No blindness blindeth any way
So thoroughly, so fully
As longing lust unruly.
Howe'er we'd pass't in silence by,
The truth of the saying we can't deny:
" Beauty killeth duty."
The wonderful, great beauty
Of Isolde blinded
By its bloom th' unminded
Mark without and within,
Eyes and soul, with such a screen,
That he could not see in her aught
What he might charge as bad ; no, nought.
All that he saw her doing
As the best shone in his knowing.
To end this matter, let me say
He loved to be with her alway
So dearly, that he overlooked
All the care and grief he from her brooked.

What in the heart lies all the time
Sealed up and closed from its first prime,
Cannot remain long hidden.
We like to do what bidden
By our thoughts to do in a matter.
The eye loves to fetter
Its sight into its pleasure.
Heart and eye, both treasure
And love to pasture on that lawn,
Where each its pleasure sees upgrown.
And who such play would seek to spoil,
God knows, makes't dearer all the while.
The more you try to drive them off,
The more they love this play of love,
And closer grasp it in their hold.
Thus did Tristan and Isolde.
As soon as this to them was done,
And all their joy and pleasure gone,
By watchful guard locked out their love,
And by command from them shut off:
Sorely seized them sorrow.
Love and longing then through
Grief first roused in them, and woe,
Aye woe more wild than e'er ; and so
They yearned toward each other
With a burning, harder to smother,
Than them before had troubled.
The mountain load redoubled
Fell on them, of the hated
Watch ; and unabated
Pressed on them like a mountain of lead.
Watchful guard — the devil-bred —

That foe of love and hater
All their mind did scatter.
Isolde chiefly languished.
She grieved and she anguished :
Tristan's estrangement was her grief.
The more her lord told her to live
No more with Tristan so intimate,
The more her thought and soul did set,
And in Tristan were buried now.
Aye, thanks to the watch for this we owe!
The watch does ever feed and bear,
Whene'er we feeding it uprear,
Nought but the haw-bush and the thorn,
This is the jealous wrath then born,
Which glory and honor takes fro' man,
And dishonors many a woman,
Who'd gladly honor nourish,
Would we her rightly cherish.
But when injustice her is showed,
She sickens in honor and in mood.
Thus has the watch perverted,
And honor and mood deserted.
And with all these tricks uncommon,
Watch is wasted on woman ;
And for this ground : because no man
With watch a bad one can restrain ;
And a good one needs no watch, for she
Watches herself, as we can see.
And who puts other watch her o'er
Grows hateful to her more and more ;
Helping merely to lower
The woman, and taking fro' her

Honor and truth so fully,
She nevermore can duly
To pure behavior now return.
There's always something will stay and burn!
'Tis even the fruit the hawthorn left.
For wheresoe'er the hawthorn daft
In such sweet ground and furrow
Took its root once through,
'Tis harder work to weed it out
Than when in the desert it does sprout.

I know well, that a noble will,
If we unjustly treat it, till
To evil fruit't at last gives birth,
Henceforth more evil fruit brings forth
Than one that's always evil been.
'Tis true, for thus I've read it e'en.
Hence should a wise man and one whom
A woman's honor is dear and home,
On a woman's doing
No watch keep e'er pursuing
In secret, or guard, other than
Kind teaching and guiding can restrain,
Tenderness and loving.
This watch ne'er-removing
He for a certainty may know
Better watch none can bestow.
For whether she good or evil is,
Does one her often injustice,
She, like enough, a mind will sprout,
Which you would gladly be without.
Nay, every brave and honest man,

Who manful mood boasts not in vain,
Should trust in his wife's purity,
And in himself have surety
That for his love and pleasure
She'll ne'er transgress the measure
However you begin it ;
From woman her love, to win it
You must not use, or force, or eke
Such evil ways as some men seek.
You'll rather quench love in this way.
Watch is in love an evil play.
It quickens anger and passion's host.
And the woman with it is surely lost.

Faith, who'd leave off these vain commands
Would certainly do well, my friends !
In women they raise scorn and scoff,
Simply to break them is pleasure enough ;
And thus we do what we never done had
Had it not been prohibited.
This very thistle and this thorn,
God knows! in woman seems inborn.
Women of this kind, who so live,
Are children of their mother Eve.
She 'twas who the first commandment broke.
Our Lord God gave her leave to pluck
Fruits and flowers and rare grass,
All that there in paradise was,
To do with it without measure
As might suit her pleasure.
But one He her prohibited
By her life and death — 'tis said

By priests this tree of Eden
Was the fig-tree all fruit-laden.
This plucked she and broke God's command,
Loosing herself and God off-hand.
It is e'en still my firm belief,
Eve never had thus come to grief,
Had not the command been on her laid.
The first work thus which e'er she made
Therewith she built up all her kind:
What was commanded she did not mind.
And when we think the matter o'er,
Eve surely could dispense this; for
Of all the fruits this woman
Could claim all in common
At her pleasure's option,
This one but the exception;
And yet she would none but this one,
And all her honor with it was gone.

Thus are they all yet children of Eve,
Who after Eve are Eved and live.
Aye who the command could issue:
How many of Eve's tissue
Could yet be found command would eke
Themselves and God most untrue make!
Now since their kind brings this with it,
And nature thus makes't in them meet:
That woman, who can above it rise
Gains praise and honor in our eyes.
For she is virtuous in spite of kind,
Who gladly in spite of kind keeps mind
Of her honor, body, and her shame.

She is a woman but by name,
And is a man in manner.
Nor should we e'er restrain her,
But all her deeds upon her
Turn to praises and honor.
Where thus a woman her womanhood
And her heart throws off and mood,
And with man's kind thus blendeth
There the pine-tree honey spendeth,
The henbane balm outfloweth ;
The nettle's root upgroweth
Into fair rose unto men.

What else indeed can woman
Bring forth of purer breeding
Than 'gainst her body's pleading
To lead her honor's forces ?
According to the resources
Of each, body and honor ?
Turning the fight upon her
So that each one gets its just due ;
Protecting each one of the two
So that the other one dies not
Neglected by her in its lot ?
She no noble woman is
Who her body her honor to please,
Or her honor for her body neglects.
She has the power, if she right acts,
To keep of both possession,
Detract from neither in passion,
But keep both retaining
In weal or woe ne'er waning,

No matter what may happen.
God knows, things must so shapen,
That she will rise in worth always.
With effort e'er remittingless
Let her by proper measure
Weigh all her life and pleasure ;
Therewith e'er garnish all her soul
Thereunder her body and arts enroll.
Measure, the pure and holy,
Body and honor guards solely.

Of all the things that in this world
The sunlight has to sight unfurled
The blessedest thing a woman is,
Who body and life, never remiss,
Doth under measure's rule e'er keep.
Who for herself feels rare love deep ;
And all the time and all the while
That she on herself with love does smile,
'Tis simply fair, that even so
The world should with love for her grow.
A woman who her own body harms,
Whose mind is turned to such vile charms,
As make her herself wrathy hate, —
Who can love her as loving mate ?
Who her own body disgraces
And all the world thus faces :
How can one love and honor
And faith pour out upon her ?
We quench whatever yearning
Had just begun heartburning.
The nameless life of love to live

With name unworthy't to receive.
No, no, that is not loving !
That is love's foe, the roving
Honorless and reckless
Evil, never speckless
That ne'er lent worth to woman's name.
A truthful proverb says the same :
" Who many's love pursueth,
The love of many undoeth ! "
Who keeps her mind e'er moving
To catch the whole world's loving :
Let her first love herself and prove
To all the world what kind her love.
Has her love genuine color,
All the world her love will follow.
A woman, who her womanhood
'Gainst her own body keepeth good,
For the world's sweet pleasure,
The whole world too should treasure,
Beautify, praise-crown her,
In wreaths and flowers drown her,
And new honoring daily,
Themselves new honor rally.
Whom such a one gives ever,
And blesses with, her favor,
Her body, and soul, and senses,
Her love and her love's trances :
Ah, such a man was born to be blest !
He was born and chosen for best
And blessedest life in every wise !
He has the living paradise
Buried in his heart's furrow.
He need ne'er fear and sorrow

That him the haw may stinging clasp
When he the flowers would fold in his grasp.
That him the thorn may pricken,
When he the rose would breaken.
There is no haw, there is no thorn ;
There never thistle wrath has born,
It cannot grow there cozy.
Peace the ever rosy
Has weeded all these things we saw,
Thorn and thistle and the haw.
Aye, in this love-paradise
On the branches see the eyes
Greening or growing nought but what
The eye is flattered to look at.
It is all perfuming,
With womanly goodness blooming.
No fruit grows there unto man
But the truth and love of woman,
Honor and glory, that reach the skies.

Aye, in such wondrous paradise
With joy so overshowered,
With May so overflowered,
A man of blessèd kind and mind
His heart's blessedness sure would find,
And see his eyes' sweet ecstasy.
Faith, worse for him it could not be
Than 'twas for Tristan and Isolde.
If he 's seized right what I have told,
He never need his own life give
The life that Tristan led to live.
For, whom a noble and virtuous wife

Gives honor, body, herself, and life,
Intrusting both unto his care:
How loving then attends she e'er
And sweet attention him bestows!
How clears she all his paths e'er thus
From thorns and from thistles
And jealous wrath's sharp bristles!
How does she heartache from him hold!
O, never any loved Isolde
Her Tristan watched with tenderer care,
I hold it true, yea everywhere,
Who close search would be giving:
Isoldes still are living
In whom he'd find in fullest bloom
All he to find had longed and come.

18

INDEX.

———◆———

Guinevere, her infidelity, the only main historical feature of the King Arthur legends, made the central point of Tennyson's Idylls, 193 ; her relation to Launcelot, 196, 199.

Hadloub, Johann, arranger of the Manessian collection of Minnesinger, 6 ; one of his own Minnesongs, 26.

Hamle, Christian von, one of his Minnesongs, 28.

Hamlet, quotation from, to illustrate pauses, 19.

Hark! I hear the Birdlets singing, Minnesong by Gottfried von Nifen, 30.

Henry VI., Emperor, one of the Minnesinger, 4 ; his death and its effects on the peace of Germany, 142.

Hildegunde, Minnesong by Walther von der Vogelweide, 137.

Hohenburg, Margrave von, one of his Watch-songs, 25.

Hohenstauffen, the glorious reign of the house, 1 ; establishment of the Swabian form of the German language under its rule, 3 ; period of peace and justice, 127.

Hymn to the Virgin, the divine Minnesong, 80.

Innocent III., Pope, refuses to recognize Frederic II. as Emperor, 142 ; fans civil war in Germany, 145 ; issues *truncos*, ostensibly in support of the Crusades, 146.

Isolde (English Ysoude, Ysodd ; French, Iseult, Iseut, Isot ; Welsh, Essylt ; Provençal Iseus ; Italian, Isotta ; in Gottfried von Strassburg's romance alternately Isot, Isote, Isolt, Isolde, as rhyme or rhythm may suggest), alluded to in one of Ulrich von Lichtenstein's poems, 184 ; her relation to Tristan rendered unnecessarily disgusting in Tennyson's version, 199 ; Gottfried's romance excites, on the contrary, our sympathy and pity for her, 200 ; no unchaste desire until the love potion is taken, 202.

Kärnten, Duke of, for a time host of Walther von der Vogelweide, but behaving rather stingily, 147.

Knight-minstrels, description of their education and life, 7.

Korineis (Korineus), Roman general, traditionary brother of Brutus, and conqueror over the giant inhabitants of ancient Britain, 228.

Kudrun, one of the two great national German epics of the Minnesinger period, 2 ; its construction in strophe-form by the bards of the people, 189.

Kurneval (Cornwales), where the Grotto of Love was situated, and Mark's kingdom, 242.

Kurvenal, in the old English poem called "Gouvernayl, his man," Tristan's tutor, friend, and companion, accompanies Tristan and Isolde to the Grotto of Love, 227 ; is sent back to court by them, 230 ; Mark dispatches him to bring Tristan and Isolde back to court, 259.

Lament, Minnesong by Walther von der Vogelweide, 159.

Latin, rhyme capacities of the language made use of by the Minnesinger, 73.

Launcelot, his relation to Queen Guinevere, 196, 199.

Lay, distinctive form of the Minnelay, 57 ; Lays of Ulrich von Wintersteten,